THE MACHINERY OF DEATH

A SHOCKING INDICTMENT OF CAPITAL PUNISHMENT IN THE UNITED STATES

AMNESTY INTERNATIONAL USA
322 Eighth Avenue
New York, NY 10001

ISBN 0-939994-94-1

Book Design and Production: Bonnie Greenfield

THE MACHINERY OF DEATH

CONTENTS

THE MACHINERY OF DEATH

THE EDITORS

ENID HARLOW Acting Director of AIUSA's Program to Abolish the Death Penalty, and former literary editor of *Harper's Bazaar*, is the author of the novel, *Crashing*, and numerous short stories.

DAVID MATAS Human rights and refugee immigration lawyer in Winnipeg, is the coordinator of the legal network of Amnesty International, Canadian Section, English-speaking branch.

JANE ROCAMORA An attorney whose clients have included death-row inmates, is a member of AIUSA's legal support network and a long-time Amnesty International human rights activist.

INTRODUCTION

THE MACHINERY OF DEATH: A SHOCKING INDICTMENT OF CAPITAL PUNISHMENT

IN AUGUST OF 1993, Amnesty International USA (AIUSA) convened a "Commission of Inquiry into the Death Penalty as Practiced in the United States." The purpose of this Commission, which brought together internationally renowned death penalty experts, was to determine whether capital punishment, as practiced in the United States, constituted a *prima facie* violation of internationally accepted legal norms. The Commission heard testimony on a wide variety of death penalty issues from a broad range of witnesses, including family members of murder victims, lawyers who represent capital defendants, former death-row inmates, and academics who have particular expertise on various aspects of the death penalty and applicable international standards.

Amnesty International believes that the death penalty, wherever practiced, violates the respect for life and the right to be free from torture and cruel, inhuman and degrading treatment or punishment. The following pages graphically illustrate the ways in which the death penalty violates these basic human rights and the human tragedies that flow from its use.

This testimony, originally delivered at AIUSA's 1993 International Council Meeting in Boston, indicts not only the death penalty in the United States, but also the death penalty wherever it is practiced. It conclusively demonstrates that the United States, even with its vast judicial resources and elaborate procedural safeguards, executes the innocent, executes youthful offenders in clear violation of international law, imposes death sentences in a racially discriminatory manner, ignores the special vulnerability of the mentally ill and those with mental retardation, and fails to provide adequate counsel for indigent capital defendants. By its very use, the death penalty violates a host of human rights standards which are central to Amnesty International's mandate.

In the following first-person accounts, readers will learn of the interplay between racism and the United States' judicial system which sent an innocent man, Walter McMillian, to Alabama's death row; they will learn how Stephen Bright, a veteran lawyer for death-row inmates, uncovered proof that the District Attorney in Columbus, Georgia, pursues death sentences on the basis of the victim's race; they will learn about an ongoing study conducted by Margaret Vandiver and William Bowers, illustrating the racist attitudes of jurors who actually sentenced African-Americans to death. While the testimony is grouped broadly according to subject, some overlap unavoidably occurs as the most egregious human rights violations inherent in the use of the death penalty are referred to again and again.

Although the level of violent crime and its severe costs to our society in human, moral and economic terms are serious issues confronting the U.S., the evidence presented before this Commission clearly demonstrates that the death penalty is neither a deterrent nor a solution to violent crime. Indeed, the testimony provided in these pages both reflects isolated instances of appalling injustice and raises disturbing questions about trends in the administration of capital punishment in the United States.

Even those who are well-informed about the practice of the death penalty in the U.S. will find shocking new information here. *The Machinery of Death* exposes the putrid inner workings of the capital punishment system. The editors hope readers will use this book for what it is, a powerful tool in the struggle for worldwide abolition.

Amnesty International wishes to thank Ashanti Chimurenga, AIUSA's former Director of the Program to Abolish the Death Penalty, for her inspiration in creating and organizing the Commission. We also would like to thank our esteemed international jurists: Lloyd Barnett, President, Jamaican Bar Association; Roger Hood, Director, Centre for Criminological Research, University of Oxford; Gitobu Imanyara, Kenyan human rights attorney and editor-in-chief, *Nairobi Weekly*; Dr. Abdul Carimo Issa, Special Advisor to the Ministry of Justice, Republic of Mozambique; Florizelle O'Connor, Director, Jamaica Council for Human Rights; Dr. Belisario dos Santos, attorney and member of the Comissao Justica e Paz da Arquidiocese de Sao Paulo; and Francis Seow, Barrister-at-Law and Visiting Fellow, East Asian Legal Studies, Harvard Law School, for having traveled long distances and given such careful attention to the witnesses as they appeared before them. Finally, we extend our thanks to Benjamin Low-Beer, Jeffrey Seaman and Deirdre McEvoy for having volunteered their time to provide additional editing and footnoting for this publication.

THE EDITORS

HENRY SCHWARZSCHILD

THE DEATH PENALTY IN THE UNITED STATES: A COMMENTARY AND REVIEW

I AM NOW the head of the New York office of the National Coalition to Abolish the Death Penalty, an organization created in 1976 to coordinate the efforts of some 60 major national religious, minority-community, civil-rights, civil-liberties, and other organizations, and a great many regional and state anti-death penalty coalitions.

We were founded as soon as the United States Supreme Court in 1976, in effect, re-opened the execution chambers in this country.[1] Before assuming that task, I had been for 15 years the director of the Capital Punishment Project of the American Civil Liberties Union, a 75-year-old human rights and civil liberties organization which defends the principles of the Bill of Rights against the intrusion of personal liberty by government.

Before that, I had been involved as a private person in the issue of the death penalty. My interest in the matter goes back a long way, perhaps primarily occasioned by the fact that, by the accidents of family, history and circumstance, I grew up in the 1920's and 30's in Nazi Germany and left there as a refugee from Hitler oppression just before World War II. I became intimately familiar with what happens when governments have the power to decide who lives and who dies.

HENRY SCHWARZSCHILD Director, New York Office of the National Coalition to Abolish the Death Penalty (NCADP). Founder, 1976: NCADP. Board Member: NCADP, Jewish Peace Fellowship, Jews for Racial and Economic Justice. Director Emeritus, Capital Punishment Project, ACLU, whose work he led for 15 years; National Advisory Committee, American-Arab Anti-discrimination Committee.

The death penalty has been available in the United States since colonial days, brought over here with European settlers and European law, and has always existed in this country. In the middle of the 19th century, a small number of states abolished the death penalty and have never reintroduced it;[2] but the majority of U.S. states have retained it.

One has to remember the criminal justice system in this country is organized such that normal criminal law problems are primarily the jurisdiction of the individual states, that there is, at the same time, a federal criminal code, but that ordinary crimes are preeminently left to the disposition of the state authorities under the state criminal laws.

Thirty-six of the 50 states that make up the United States of America have death penalty laws on their books.[3] Fourteen and the District of Columbia do not.[4] Given the trend we see now, it is unlikely that more than a few additional states will enact new death penalty laws.

The federal criminal code has the death penalty available; and so does the military code, applicable only to military personnel. Both codes are enacted by the federal Congress of the United States. In these 36 states and these two federal jurisdictions, there are almost 3,000 people under sentence of death, awaiting the knock of the executioner on their cell door.[5] We add to this number at a rate of somewhere between 200 and 250 a year. We have not in recent years executed more than about 30 people a year, which falls far short of the number of death sentences imposed, but the number of annual executions is rising steadily.

The largest number of executions in one year in this country came in 1935 when the United States executed 199 people.[6] We now sentence more people to death than that in a year, but the rate of executions has been retarded by the complex criminal justice system, which involves both state and federal courts, and a whole series of other circumstances.

It was not until the 1960's, in the context of the great civil-rights revolution, that the issue of the federal constitutionality of the death penalty under the Eighth Amendment of the Constitution, which prohibits cruel and unusual punishment, was first raised in our courts. A case was taken ultimately to the United States Supreme Court in the late 60's and early 70's, essentially on three related grounds: that the arbitrariness, the unpredictability, the illogic of the imposition of the death penalty and of executions violated the Due Process Clause of the Fifth and Fourteenth Amendments; that the racially discriminatory use of the death penalty violated the Equal Protection Clause of the Fourteenth Amendment; and that in any event, the death penalty ought, in an enlightened and civilized society, to be recognized as cruel and unusual punishment and therefore barred by the federal Constitution.

...in any event, the death penalty ought, in an enlightened and civilized society, to be recognized as cruel and unusual punishment and therefore barred by the federal Constitution.

When those claims reached the United States Supreme Court in 1972 in a case called *Furman v. Georgia*,[7] the Supreme Court, in a complex series of plurality holdings, held that the death penalty was both discriminatory (such as to violate the Equal Protection Clause of the federal Constitution) and arbitrary and irrational (so as to violate the Due Process Clause) and that so applied and so imposed, the death penalty was indeed cruel and unusual punishment.[8] That was a radical, revolutionary victory.

There were some 600 or so men and women on death row at that point, all of whom the Supreme Court said, in effect, had been sentenced to death under unconstitutional statutes and were thus out from under a death judgment. There was then, by virtue of this Supreme Court holding, no valid death penalty statute anywhere in the United States, either on the state or federal statute books.

But as both the state legislatures and we who were concerned with this matter reflected more closely upon the Supreme Court decision, it appeared very quickly that the Court had not said the death penalty was *inherently* a violation of the federal Constitution, but only when imposed in an arbitrary and discriminatory manner. The Supreme Court judgment traced the arbitrariness and discriminatoriness in the use of capital punishment to the fact that under those statutes, it was left essentially to the discretion of the sentencer, usually the judge, sometimes with some participatory recommendation power of the jury, to decide whether in this particular case the appropriate sentence would be life or death. The exercise of that absolute sentencing discretion in capital cases was, the Supreme Court suggested, what had led to both arbitrariness and discriminatoriness.

In the three or four years immediately subsequent to *Furman*, states reenacted new death penalty statutes. Some of them wrote mandatory death penalty laws under which a defendant, if convicted of a capital offense, would be automatically sentenced to death.[9] There was no discretion in the sentencing and therefore no abuse of that discretion by way of arbitrariness or discriminatoriness. In that manner these states hoped to overcome the Supreme Court's objections.

Other states enacted what came to be called "guided-discretion statutes" in which the law provided a second proceeding after the trial in which evidence would be presented in aggravation of that particular crime and in mitigation. The jury then would make findings on aggravation and mitigation, weigh those considerations, and in light of them somehow make a judgment as to whether the appropriate sentence would be death or life.

Under these new kinds of death-penalty statutes enacted subsequent to 1972, some hundreds of people were sentenced to death. The new statutes were again challenged for their constitutionality. In 1976, in *Gregg v. Georgia*, the Supreme Court provided us with the legal framework for capital punishment in which we operate to this day.[10] The Court held that the new, post-*Furman* mandatory death-penalty laws were invalid, just as were the absolutely discretionary death-penalty laws before them. The Court held to be constitutional the new guided-discretion death-penalty laws because those gave promise of avoiding the arbitrariness and the discriminatoriness in death judgments to which they had objected four years earlier.

We believe the death penalty to be a morally intolerable institution. We believe that governments ought not to have the legal power and do not possess the moral right to decide who lives and who dies. We believe governments may not use homicide as an instrument of social policy.

Yet the evidence is abundant and irrefutable and has not been challenged even by this United States Supreme Court that the imposition of the death penalty under post-1976 law continues to be precisely as arbitrary, as irrational, and as discriminatory as it was before the Supreme Court announced its 1972 decisions.[11] But the Court, for political reasons, is very much more conservative about this and declines to entertain that claim. In its commitment to retain the death penalty, the Court has declined to entertain the irrevocable and massive criminological, sociological, legal evidence for the failings of death-penalty laws under its own standards.[12]

When the issue is whether the government may kill a human being, there is no reliability sufficient to justify that. I would not find it justifiable if that reliability were available, because I believe that no society can truly call itself civilized that uses premeditated violent homicide as an instrument of social policy; but it seems to me useless to talk about a hypothetical society in which the death penalty is applied rationally, predictably, fairly, without error, without discrimination. Such a society does not exist here and is unlikely ever to exist. In any real society, the death penalty ought to be eliminated because human beings are fallible.

Government surely is not entitled to kill innocent people—no one dissents from that—but in our judgment, governments ought not to be in the business of killing any human beings.

I think the anti-death penalty movement in this country is surprisingly strong in its institutional base and surprisingly weak in its popular and political one. We believe the death penalty to be a morally intolerable institution. We believe that governments ought not to have the legal power and do not possess the moral right to decide who lives and who dies. We believe governments may not use homicide as an instrument of social policy. Even if it were possible to administer the death penalty in a fair, equitable, nondiscriminatory, and error-free fashion, the death penalty would violate fundamental human rights.

NOTES

[1] *Gregg v. Georgia*, 428 U.S. 153 (1976).
[2] Hugo Bedau, *The Death Penalty in America*, 3rd edition, Oxford University Press, 1982, p.21. Between the 1840's and the 1870's, Iowa, Maine, Michigan, Rhode Island and Wisconsin abolished the death penalty and have not reintroduced it.
[3] On July 1, 1994, Kansas became the 37th U.S. state with a death penalty statute.
[4] See supra, note 3.
[5] NAACP Legal Defense and Educational Fund, Inc., *Death Row, U.S.A.* (Winter 1993).
[6] U.S. Department of Justice, *Bureau of Justice Statistics Bulletin: Capital Punishment 1991*, p.12.
[7] 408 U.S. 238 (1972).
[8] Ibid.
[9] *Roberts v. Louisiana*, 428 U.S. 325 (1976). *Woodson v. North Carolina*, 428 U.S. 280 (1976).
[10] See supra, note 1.
[11] *McCleskey v. Kemp*, 481 U.S. 279 (1987).
[12] Ibid.

ASHANTI CHIMURENGA

THE SHAME OF THE DEATH PENALTY

THE DEATH PENALTY is a violation of humanitarian standards, the United States Constitution, U.S. state constitutions, and it is an intolerable disrespect for all people and represents the most gross disrespect for human life.

The death penalty has historically played a role in the United States, particularly in former slave-holding states. The *Dred Scott Decision*[1], which stated emphatically that a black person was not a human being of a hundred percent worth, reflected the worst of what the U.S. Supreme Court could do, which was to defile the very notion of a human being. More than a hundred years later, in 1987, the United States Supreme Court ruled in *McCleskey*[2] that racism was inevitable in a criminal justice system, and to that degree sanctioned it, and allowed Warren McCleskey to be executed, as it has allowed so many others to be. There certainly have been high points within the American system of democracy, stars to reach toward; but we must be grounded, and we must look at the reality of the death penalty today.

On July 30, 1992, a man named William Andrews was executed in Utah.[3] In his case the jury produced a note that said, "Hang the nigger." The note showed a man hanging from a tree. Seventy-two judges within these United States of America and through countless appellate courts determined that Andrews was not entitled to even an evidentiary hearing on the question of whether such a

ASHANTI CHIMURENGA is an attorney and a former Director of AIUSA's Program to Abolish the Death Penalty.

note and such an action constituted racism or prejudiced his right to a fair trial.[4] The death penalty is a form of state-sanctioned lynching; and that, reputedly, comes out of the mouth of former U.S. Supreme Court Justice Thurgood Marshall.

As late as January 1993, the United States Supreme Court ruled it was constitutional to execute an innocent person, as long as such a manifest injustice was preceded by something called a 'fair trial,' within the notion of a criminal justice system that would not understand fairness if it walked in the door.[5]

The necessity for international standards, international review, international attention, international monitoring of the death penalty in the United States is critical. U.S. institutions have abandoned and retreated from their obligation to uphold the law. They have done so out of gross disrespect for all human life, but in particular they have manifested this disrespect for the poor of all colors, the weak, and those with mental retardation.

We must, on behalf of the 2800 people on death row, on behalf of Curtis and Danny Harris, two blood brothers, ripped from a family within one month and with little attention, stop the United States from killing, killing, killing in our name, because that is exactly what this country is doing, and we are authorizing it. We must not stay quiet.

The cases abound. One was a young black man who encompassed all of the problems of a youth with mental retardation from an impoverished background, who was also a juvenile offender, and was executed by the state of Louisiana.[6] Another was Johnny Garrett in Texas, severely abused, mentally incapacitated, and executed.[7] Continuously and repeatedly, U.S. courts and state courts abandon doctrines. The doctrine of the right to confront witnesses, the right to a fair trial, to an impartial injury, due process, equal protection, balanced punishment, punishment that fits the crime are standards and terms that mean nothing in this country.

We stand together in a pool of blood, and the burden is on each one of us to stop this death penalty, this killing machine that traumatizes us all. In the course of that, we will move forward for all of those who have been executed. We will strike forward toward the day that another young black person will not be executed with a "hang the nigger" note around his neck, and there won't be another poor, impoverished white youth like Johnny Garrett sent to his death.

United States arrogance toward international standards has been the barrier. That barrier must come down because the death penalty is of concern to all individuals all over the world. We must unite around this issue now, not tomorrow. We must, on behalf of the 2800 people on death row, on behalf of Curtis and Danny Harris,[8] two blood brothers, ripped from a family within one month and with little attention, stop the United States from killing, killing, killing in our name, because that is exactly what this country is doing, and we are authorizing it. We must not stay quiet.

The death penalty violates every standard of law, every standard of humanitarian justice, and every vision that we may have of what human beings and humanity must represent in this country and all over the world.

NOTES

[1] *Dred Scott v. Stanford*, 60 U.S. (19 How.) 393 (1857).

[2] *McCleskey v. Kemp*, 481 U.S. 279 (1987).

[3] William Andrews, executed July 30, 1992, Utah, NAACP Legal Defense and Educational Fund, Inc., *Execution Update*, August 3, 1994.

[4] *Petition Alleging Violations of the Human Rights of William Andrews by the United States of America and the State of Utah*, LDF Capital Punishment Project, New York, NY, International Human Rights Clinic, Washington College of Law, The American University, Washington, D.C., submitted July 28, 1992.

[5] *Herrera v. Collins*, U.S. Supreme Court, decided January 25, 1993.

[6] Dalton Prejean, executed May 18, 1990, Louisiana. LDF, *Execution Update*, August 3, 1994.

[7] Johnny Garrett, executed February 11, 1992, Texas. LDF, *Execution Update*, August 3, 1994.

[8] Curtis Harris, executed July 1, 1993, Texas; Danny Harris, executed July 30, 1993, Texas. LDF, *Execution Update*, August 3, 1994.

KEITH JENNINGS

U.S. DEATH PENALTY: A LEGACY OF SLAVERY

IT IS IMPORTANT for us especially as we consider the issue of the death penalty in the United States to ground our thoughts in a proper historical perspective.

The history of capital punishment is not only a legal history. The social context around it begins even before the founding of this country. Along with the coming of European settlers to the North American continent came a certain set of laws and codes. Because that set of laws would eventually include the enslavement of millions of African peoples and the physical elimination of millions of indigenous peoples, punishment and the law have always been associated with social control and the maintenance of white supremacy.

The historic legacies of injustice, lynching, police brutality, peonage, the denial of civil and political rights and racial discrimination in the use of public and private facilities all have their roots in the settler community and slave society established on the North American continent. The physical dispossession, persecution, torture, genocide, social and mental attitudes fostered by enslavement and

KEITH JENNINGS is Executive Director of The African-American Human Rights Foundation, a Washington, D.C.-based organization dedicated to human rights education and to documenting and researching human rights violations in the United States. Mr. Jennings has traveled extensively throughout the Americas, Africa, Asia and Europe, speaking at international meetings on peace, social justice and the need to eliminate all forms of racial discrimination. He has testified before the U.N. Special Committee on Apartheid and has represented the African-American human rights community at the 1986 World Peace Congress in Copenhagen, and at the 1993 Vienna U.N. World Conference on Human Rights.

colonialism would immediately be seen today as violations of human rights.

A persistent thread running through the fabric of the American experience is racial discrimination. Racism is deeply rooted in the history and social structure of the United States of America. Race is the American trauma.

Racism in doctrine and practice is a concoction developed firstly, to justify enslavement of African peoples and the genocide committed against indigenous peoples in the Americas, and secondly, to justify the establishment of a colonial system. The practice of racism, as an action, has the effect of nullifying or impairing the recognition, enjoyment or exercise of human rights and fundamental freedoms in certain fields solely based on race. Racism as a practice was first administered on a mass scale to overcome the resistance to the introduction and maintenance of slavery.

Slavery in the United States was a labor system based upon the capture and bondage of human beings from Africa, their shipment, sale and subsequent employment in the economy as human machines, work animals, sold and resold as chattel commodities on a capitalist market. The apologist of the slave merchants and cotton growers shamelessly developed the doctrine of the inherent supremacy of people of "white skin" and the inherent inferiority of people of "black skin."

In colonial America, even those Europeans willing to make a revolution in pursuit of their rights were able to ignore the human rights and fundamental freedoms of their darker brothers and sisters. The founding fathers went even further. In attempting to excommunicate the African people from the human race, they removed any need to respect their dignity as members of the human race.

In order to be successful at establishing a "more perfect union" where freedom was equated with free enterprise and where property rights could not be abridged by the state, the founders of this country created a strong central government and considered Africans, my ancestors, to be three-fifths of a person for purposes of representation.

The development of "slave codes," which varied from place to place, generally forbade the enslaved African to leave the plantation without a pass, to carry weapons, to strike a Christian, to learn to read or write, to associate with free Africans, or even to play the drum.[1] Punishment for violations of the code included flogging, being branded in the face with a hot iron, being maimed in a variety of ways such as having one's ears cut off.[2] Noted historian, Dr. John Hope Franklin, has argued:

> *The invention of instruments of torture must have taxed the ingenuity of those in command. There was the tronco constructed of wood or iron, by which the slave's ankles were fastened in one place for several days; the libambo did the same thing to the arms. The novenas and trezenas were devices by which a slave was tied face down, and beaten for nine or thirteen consecutive nights.*[3]

It was the civil war and the passage of the 13th, 14th, and 15th Amendments to the United States Constitution that officially ended slavery in the U.S.A. Although slavery was abolished by the 13th Amendment (except for prisoners) in the latter decades of the 19th century, all southern states and many others passed "Black Codes" or "Jim Crow" laws mandating racial segregation in almost all areas of public life and different treatment in both private and public affairs.

Political economist, Thomas Boston, has pointed out:

> *Legally, "Black Codes" were enacted. These laws prohibited labor migration, regulated working conditions on the old plantations, established harsh penalties for vagrancy and in some cases prohibited Blacks from purchasing land. Their fundamental intent was to shackle the freed slave to the old plantations, abolish labor market competition, consolidate the new system of labor and reestablish the economic supremacy of the defeated slave oligarchy.*[4]

In effect, "Jim Crow" laws once again legalized and legislated white supremacy and white domination throughout the society for all national minorities and indigenous peoples who existed outside any constitutional protection. Segregation and the reservation system established an American Apartheid system that in 1948 white South Africans would come to the United States to study and emulate.

The overthrow of reconstruction was complete as the federal government interpreted in *Plessy v. Ferguson* that separate but equal was constitutional. American Apartheid became a fact of life for all people of color across the country. For African-Americans:

> *Voting rights were rescinded and property rights attacked. Blacks were driven legally and forcibly out of local, state and federal political offices. By 1901 there was not a single Black elected to a federal office.... A vicious but legally sanctioned era of Jim Crow segregation was about to begin.*[5]

To economically maintain this new system of oppression, the forced labor system set up after slavery gave way to a new system of exploitation of tenant farming. The vast majority of tenant farmers were sharecroppers. This designation insured that African-Americans would be relegated to the lowest segment of the labor market.[6]

In the event that African-Americans objected to their position within the society they were "lynched." According to John Hope Franklin, in the last sixteen years of the 19th century more than 2,500 lynchings took place, the great majority of which were of African-Americans. During the first part of the 20th century, before the First World War, the number reached more than 1,100.[7]

"Jim Crow" segregation was an official government policy violently enforced. In practice, it violated the most basic human rights and fundamental freedoms. The main ingredient for the restoration of white supremacy was the disenfranchisement of African-Americans. The white view was clearly stated by J.K. Vardaman of Mississippi when he said:

> *I am just as opposed to Booker Washington as a voter, with all his Anglo-Saxon re-enforcements, as I am to the coconut-headed, chocolate-colored, typical little coon,*

> *Andy Dotson, who blacks my shoes every morning. Neither is fit to perform the supreme function of citizenship.*[8]

"Black Codes" were a set of legalized punishments that differentiated between people of color on one side and whites on the other. The classic example of this different treatment before the law was the issue of rape. If a black woman was raped, the punishment might have been a $25 fine. If a white woman was raped, the punishment was a mandatory death sentence.[9] Rape has been a key feature of the capital punishment system, legally and extra-legally. In Georgia, the state I am from, between 1924 and 1972, there were 412 people executed for rape; 337 were African-American men.[10]

It was not until 1954 that the "separate but equal" doctrine was successfully challenged by civil rights groups and overturned by the Supreme Court. The dynamic civil rights movement, led by African-Americans, gave rise to the 1964 Civil Rights Act, the 1965 Voting Rights Act and the 1968 Fair Housing Act. In addition to that body of law, a number of agencies was established to insure that all Americans received equality before the law. However, the anti-discrimination law of the United States, while good in theory, in practice lacks enforcement and increasingly is ignored altogether.

The issue of capital punishment perhaps best typifies the institutionalized racist violence committed against poor people in the U.S.A., especially African-Americans. Forty-one percent of the U.S. death-row population is African-American. Another nine percent is composed of national minorities from other racial groups. Of all those executed since executions began again in 1977, more than 85 percent have been killed for killing whites. And of the more than 250 people executed, only one white has been killed for murdering an African-American.[11] At the federal level, 75 percent of the persons sentenced to death have been African-Americans.[12]

Today, Georgia is about 30 percent black; however, 70 percent of the people in its prisons are black.[13] Georgia's elected Attorney General, Michael Bowers, says that racism has nothing to do with the death penalty in Georgia. But what is the history of Georgia on the execution of men convicted of raping women? The oldest per-

We have a saying in the African-American human rights movement that capital punishment in the United States has been reserved for those without capital.

son executed in Georgia was 72. He was black. The youngest person executed in Georgia was 13. He was black. The only woman ever executed in Georgia was black. The highest number of people ever executed in Georgia at one time was six; they were all black.[14] So, I put this question to the Attorney General: If you were a capital defendant on trial for killing a black person, how would you feel if you had an all-black jury, a hostile black District Attorney, a black judge? Why should any African-American or any other person of color accept these conditions? Why should any African-American person accept unfair trials where an individual who is against the death penalty is barred from serving on a jury; where prosecutors are allowed to exclude people of color from juries?

We have a saying in the African-American human rights movement that capital punishment in the United States has been reserved for those without capital. This maxim remains true, even today. Capital punishment raises economic, class-based prejudices because of the complex issue of legal representation for the poor. In the New South, most indigent defense attorneys receive between $500 and $1500 to do maybe seven hundred hours of the lawyering needed for the trial of a capital case. These circumstances regularly result in severely inadequate representation.

Effective representation has become a central issue in capital cases over the last twelve years because the United States Supreme Court has launched an assault on the rights of criminal defendants, raising serious human rights concerns. The Supreme Court has essentially held that it will not concern itself with the alarming information showing race discrimination in capital cases.

I emphasize the role of the courts in this issue. If you are an African-American caught up in the criminal justice system in the United States, your chances of seeing someone who looks like you are minimal. Judges and prosecutors are, for the most part, white.

There are more than 12,000 trial lawyers in the U.S.A. About 140 of them are black.[15] Many of these black lawyers are of the mind-set of Supreme Court Justice Clarence Thomas. I am not lying when I say it. Some of the people who sit on the bench maintain a white supremacist mentality. In sum, considering the entire context in which capital punishment operates in the U.S., I would say that there is a criminal justice crisis in this country.

Political opportunism dominates the issue of capital punishment in this country. Two days ago the Republicans in Congress filed a bill calling for expanded use of the death penalty, speedier executions, and expanded use of mandatory sentences as criminal punishments. Democrats in Congress responded, filing legislation which called for essentially the same things because the Democratic Party has decided it will never again be beaten on law and order policy issues by the Republicans.[16] In another example, in 1992, Bill Clinton, as a candidate for the Presidency of the United States, left the campaign trail, returned to his home state of Arkansas, and ordered the execution of an essentially brain-dead black man. That man, Ricky Ray Rector, should never have been on death row, but Candidate Clinton wanted to show the nation that he was tough on crime. Rather than commute his sentence, Mr. Clinton executed him.

The United States needs to do something about crime, but the context in which the policy-makers and the judiciary operate tragically prevents us from taking effective measures. The facts and circumstances I have described imply severe violations of the customary law that the Universal Declaration of Human Rights was intended to codify. They also violate specifically Articles 6 & 7 of the International Covenant on Civil and Political Rights which the U.S. recently ratified. They violate the spirit of the American Convention on Human Rights which the United States has signed but

---

...right now we have law and order in this society, but without justice...if the justice system wants people to respect the social contract we have in this society, it ought to respect the dignity of all people.

---

not ratified, and they violate the 14th Amendment of the United States Constitution, requiring equality before the law.

These things, taken together, mean that right now we have law and order in this society, but without justice. In 1835, Alexis de Tocqueville, in analyzing this experiment called "democracy," concluded that it held one danger, a tyranny of the majority.[17] I dare say that the danger he predicted is what we are facing today. I say also that if the justice system wants people to respect the social contract we have in this society, it ought to respect the dignity of all people. If it does not, we will have more riots like those which occurred in Los Angeles during the summer of 1992.

NOTES

[1] John Hope Franklin, *From Slavery to Freedom: A History of Negro Americans*, New York, McGraw-Hill, 6th edition, 1988, pp. 53-63.

[2] Ibid.

[3] Ibid., p. 51.

[4] Thomas D. Boston, *Race, Class and Conservatism*, London: UNWIN, 1988, p. 26.

[5] Boston, p. 26.

[6] Ibid.

[7] Franklin, p. 237. See also Ida B. Wells, *Struggle for Justice.*

[8] Franklin, p. 238.

[9] Thomas Boston, op. cit. See also, Mary Berry, *Black Resistance, White Law: A History of Constitutional Racism in America*, New York, Penguin Press, 1994.

[10] ACLU Death Penalty Report on Georgia, 1987; Southern Center for Human Rights, Georgia Report.

[11] *Death Row USA*, New York, NAACP Legal Defense and Educational Fund, February 1994.

[12] "Racial Disparities in Federal Death Penalty Prosecutions, 1988-1994," Staff Report by the Subcommittee on Civil and Constitutional Rights, House Committee on the Judiciary, 103rd Congress, 2nd Session, March 1994, p.6.

[13] *Americans Behind Bars*, Edna McConnell Clark Foundation, New York, April 1993, p.2.

[14] ACLU Death Penalty Report on Georgia.

[15] Ibid.

[16] The Federal Crime Bill was passed by the U.S. Congress on August 25, 1994.

[17] Alexis de Tocqueville, *Democracy in America*, 1835.

FRANK SOLOMON

INTERNATIONAL STANDARDS AND THE DEATH PENALTY

I AM AN ATTORNEY at law by profession. I come from the Republic of Trinidad and Tobago. I have practiced for a number of years in a number of human rights organizations, many of which are now defunct. Some of these became defunct, it is argued benignly on behalf of their ex-members, because there was a diminution in the amount of work required of them. Unhappily, the National Commission for the Abolition of the Death Penalty in Trinidad and Tobago cannot become defunct for that reason, because the death penalty in Trinidad and Tobago is not, by any means, obsolete.

The death penalty in any part of the world is a matter of international concern. Whether the victims are located in Abyssinia, in Iran, in Barbados, in Texas, it is a matter which is not an abstract postulate of propaganda, but an emotional and psychological fact. It is a matter which affects all humankind. And I think it is for that reason that international standards with respect to the practice of the death penalty have been developed and promoted, because it would seem that there can be no other justification for the development through international institutions of standards which relate specifically to matters of municipal law and which trespass into the sovereignty

FRANK DAVID SOLOMON Barrister/Attorney-at-law (Port-of-Spain, Trinidad and Tobago); Head of Chambers, 1985-present; three-time past President of Bar Association of Trinidad and Tobago. Mr. Solomon was Legal Advisor to the Prime Minister of Trinidad and Tobago at both the Conference on International Criminal Law, Siracusa, Italy, and the Forty-Fifth Session of the United Nations General Assembly, New York. He is currently a member of the Bars of Trinidad and Tobago, Barbados, Grenada, St. Vincent, Guyana and the United Kingdom.

The death penalty in any part of the world is a matter of international concern. Whether the victims are located in Abyssinia, in Iran, in Barbados, in Texas, it is a matter which is not an abstract postulate of propaganda, but an emotional and psychological fact.

of nation states. There can be no other justification for the United Nations or the Organization of American States (organizations which are founded upon the respect for the individual state's sovereign rights) even discussing the death penalty. There can be no justification, other than that the practice of the death penalty touches all of humanity and so extends beyond national boundaries.

The international standards which have developed out of these international organizations, be they global or regional, are restrictive. It's an extremely tricky business to attempt to develop standards for the practice of something which substantively is unacceptable, because there is always the possibility that parties wishing to perform the unacceptable will accurately be able to say they have fully performed the standards which restricted their practice of it. So that when you have an international standard which says you may not practice the death penalty against a child, it does not mean if the accused person is not a child, you may practice the death penalty against that person.

I think it is important that we separate the legal implications of international standards from the political genesis of those standards. International standards were generated out of hard negotiation between those representatives of humankind who were repelled at the idea of the death penalty and those representatives of the same group who found it acceptable and, indeed, possibly even attractive. So the formulations you get are the result of hard bargaining and represent the lowest common denominator of acceptable human behavior by the international community.

When the United States (incontrovertibly a leading member of the international community) violates those standards, it is practicing a form of conduct lower than the lowest common denominator of acceptable human behavior agreed upon among civilized nations. It does not mean if the United States succeeds, through the meticulous observation of legal technicalities and procedure and regulations, to meet those standards, it is justified in performing judicial homicide.

It seems to me the overriding preambular statement is one which speaks of the desirability of all states moving towards the universal abolition of the death penalty. And that particular declaration means two things in the moral and political observance of international standards. It means a state may not act in a manner which goes against the general tenet of the international standards. It may not, therefore, reintroduce the death penalty once it has abolished it because that would go against the declaration of the desirability of accomplishing universal abolition. And for states which still practice the death penalty, it would mean also that they may not extend the crimes for which the death penalty is an available punishment.

It means that you may not diminish the procedural safeguards which already exist in your criminal justice system. And it means also—and I think this is fundamental—that you may not diminish the criteria of humanity that condemns a person who is entitled to have it in his favor by clemency committees and by executive pardons. It means, therefore, that these standards must be regarded strategically as beachheads from which only further progress grows, and universal abolition may proceed. You may not abandon those beachheads and still claim to be a fully paid-up member of the civilized world.

In Trinidad and Tobago we last performed an execution in 1979.[1] Since then there has been an annually increasing accumulation of persons on death row, which now amounts to a total of over 130 persons out of a population of just over 1.2 million souls. So you have a fairly large percentage of the population waiting to be killed by the rest of the nation. The reason there has been no execution since 1979 is not that successive governments have desired it to be so.

Quite the contrary. The reason is that in 1979 the human rights movements in Trinidad and Tobago took inspiration from what was going on in the rest of the world, but, in particular, from what was occurring at that time in the United States. That was the time when *Furman v. Georgia*[2] was established, and there was a juridical abolition of the death penalty *de facto*.

They did the right thing for the wrong reason, but it was accomplished. The reasons weren't looked into, but the technique, the legal technology, of examining your Constitution and extending its meanings was adopted; and, as a consequence, loopholes were found, and the issues were joined in Trinidad to the extent that executions can only take place in Trinidad today if the Constitution is changed by parliament. Of course, no parliament wishes to confront that issue, it being so inflammatory, and therefore, the stalemate remains. It's not a happy situation, but it certainly is an advance on what existed theretofore.

The death penalty is the single most important human rights issue existing today in the United States and anywhere else, for that matter, because it touches upon the philosophical choices people must make with respect to the terms under which they wish to live. What happens in the United States is of profound effect, particularly to those states who are closest to the United States and who enjoy or suffer from or certainly experience an inordinately powerful cultural influence. It was an influence for good in 1979, to us. Similarly, it is an influence for evil today. We have recently had the obscene example of the Attorney General of St. Vincent and the Grenadines, a state with a population of just over 68,000 people, calling openly for the execution of minors, obviously under the inspiration of what is going on in the United States today.

Let us move forward together. Let us not hesitate to recognize that the problem is genuinely a non-national one of global dimensions. And let us feel confident in holding hands and powerfully resisting the forces of violence, and espousing the forces of a more generous method of solution for our problems.

NOTES

[1] On July 14, 1994, Glen Ashby was hanged by the government of Trinidad and Tobago. This was the first execution in that country since 1979, and was carried out literally while the Court of Appeal was in session, hearing arguments on the constitutionality of the intended execution, and after the Court had informed the Privy Council that the execution would not be carried out before all appeals had been completed.

[2] 408 U.S. 238 (1972).

WILLIAM A. SCHABAS

INTERNATIONAL LAW AND THE DEATH PENALTY

I AM A PROFESSOR of criminal law and of human rights law at the University of Quebec at Montreal. I am also a member of the Quebec bar where I am currently defending an individual who is subject to extradition to the United States where he will face the death penalty. He is in what we in Canada call "Death Row North." I have recently published a book on the abolition of the death penalty in international law which deals with the development of international norms, and the interpretations given to them by various international and domestic tribunals.[1]

A list of abolitionist and retentionist countries prepared by Amnesty International demonstrates that 90 states have now abolished the death penalty either *de jure* or *de facto* and that 103 still retain the death penalty.[2] It also indicates that the trend is toward abolition. Approximately two countries per year abolish the death penalty. This would indicate that by the year 2000, the majority of the states in this world will have abolished the death penalty, at least in time of peace. What the list does not provide, which I

WILLIAM SCHABAS Professor of Law, University of Quebec at Montreal, specializes in criminal and human rights law. Author of: *The Abolition of the Death Penalty in International Law*, 1993; *International Human Rights Law and the Canadian Charter*, 1991. Member: International Commission of Inquiry into Human Rights Abuses in Rwanda (mission to Rwanda, January 4-21, 1993); Société Québeçoise du droit international (sécretaire-general, 1992-present); vice-president, 1990-1992; rapporteur special on the U.N. Decade of International Law, 1990-present). Mr. Schabas is also a member of the Quebec Bar, and has been involved in litigation concerning extradition from Canada to the United States of death-row inmates.

...by the year 2000, the majority of the states in this world will have abolished the death penalty, at least in time of peace.

think is also a very significant figure, is the number of states which have undertaken to abolish the death penalty at international law, as an international law issue, and not just a domestic legal issue.

These states now number 42.[3] This is a result of three international instruments. The American Convention on Human Rights,[4] which came into force in 1978, is the first abolitionist norm, because it says in Article 4 that any state which has already abolished the death penalty cannot reinstate it; and as most of the states parties to the American Convention (these are states south of the Rio Grande River) have already abolished the death penalty, they are then, at international law, abolitionist states.

The second international instrument is the Sixth Protocol to the European Convention on Human Rights,[5] which came into force in 1985 and which, in effect, represents what is now virtually a consensus of European states, something that has been recognized subsequently by the European Court of Human Rights.[6] For all intents and purposes, we can speak of Europe as being an abolitionist continent; and it can be demonstrated that this is now not only a conventional norm, but also a customary norm, of international human rights law, at least as far as Western Europe is concerned.

Finally, there is the Second Optional Protocol to the International Covenant on Civil and Political Rights.[7] This Second Optional Protocol, adopted within the United Nations human rights system, is open to virtually all states in the world for ratification (all members of the United Nations, at any rate). It demonstrates as well the enormous significance in international human rights law that has been given to the abolition of the death penalty: it is the only issue which the United Nations has specifically addressed in the context of the International Covenant, the principal international human rights treaty, as needing an amending protocol—a protocol that would change it. The Second Optional Protocol permits states to say that, in the context of all of their international human rights obligations, they insist upon the abolition of the death penalty as being part of that group of norms.

In the early international human rights instruments, provision was made for the death penalty. It was recognized as an exception to the right to life. The story in international human rights law begins with the Universal Declaration of Human Rights adopted by the United Nations General Assembly in 1948.[8] When the drafters of the Universal Declaration—Eleanor Roosevelt, Rene Cassin, John Humphrey—began work on the Universal Declaration, they had no model to follow. So they assembled all of the world's constitutions and made a kind of catalogue, sorting them by rights. Of course they found due process rights in most of the constitutions; and they found the abolition of slavery in many of the constitutions. They found the recognition of equality and opposition of racial discrimination in most of the constitutions. They also identified a right to life; but what they really found was a right to life as it is recognized in the United States Constitution,[9] that is, the right to life except in the execution of a sentence pronounced by a court. Some would say it was not a right to life at all, but in fact the recognition of the legitimacy of the death penalty.

What the drafters of the Universal Declaration of Human Rights did—and this is quite clear in the preliminary work of the Universal Declaration—was to propose that a right to life not be identified in the same fashion as it was in the United States Constitution; in other words, a right to life except in execution of a sentence. And Eleanor Roosevelt is on record as taking the view that the right to life should not be associated with the death penalty, an exception other members of the United Nations took as well.

The drafters crafted a right to life that makes no mention of the death penalty—a right to life that stands alone. Although I do not think one can argue that in 1948 there was a consensus in the United Nations, or in the world, that the death penalty be abolished, I believe it can be demonstrated that the Universal Declaration of Human Rights foresees as a common standard for mankind the abolition of the death penalty. This was followed up upon in the subsequent treaties which gave legal substance to Article 3, the right to life article of the Universal Declaration of Human Rights.

The European Convention on Human Rights,[10] adopted in 1950, went back to the old pattern because the European countries (fresh from the war crimes trials in Europe at the time) were not prepared to recognize the abolition of the death penalty. But within seven years, in 1957—(although those who are familiar with the International Covenant will note that it was adopted in 1966 and came into force in 1976)—the General Assembly finished drafting Article 6 of the International Covenant on Civil and Political Rights.[11] The International Covenant went much further than the European Convention because it limited and restricted the death penalty. It limited the application of the death penalty by saying it could not be imposed for juvenile offenses or on pregnant women. It required that the death penalty be confined only to the most serious crimes. And, in addition, it added a very loaded word, namely, that the death penalty could not be imposed "arbitrarily."

These are very important developments because they provide for a dynamic interpretation of the International Covenant. It enables us to find new abolitionist norms in Article 6, which apparently recognizes the possibility of the death penalty. As a demonstration of this, I often give the example of the execution of the insane.

The United States Supreme Court has determined quite clearly that the execution of the insane is unconstitutional.[12] Virtually every country in the world prohibits the execution of the insane. Yet it does not appear in Article 6 of the International Covenant, and it should be there. It should be there next to juveniles, next to pregnant women. But it is not. Where can it be found? Obviously, in the Covenant. I submit it is found in that word "arbitrarily," which appears in Article 6, Paragraph 1, of the International Covenant.

Finally—and this was a concession to those states which insisted that the International Covenant provide clearly for abolition—the International Covenant states that it shall not be used to impede or to prevent the abolition of the death penalty.[13] This is an important provision because the International Covenant is set out as a legal norm. Yet here we find in it something which bears a striking similarity to what is found in the Universal Declaration: an objective, a goal of humanity—abolition of the death penalty.

Three very recent and specific international law issues have been raised that concern the death penalty. The first is the International War Crimes Tribunal. In May of 1993, the United Nations Security Council set up an International Commission for the trial of war crimes in the former Yugoslavia. The statute of that tribunal, as adopted by the United Nations Security Council, specifically provides that the death penalty is not an option; in other words, the options that are available go up to imprisonment but do not include the death penalty.[14] I believe the American diplomats were in favor of including the death penalty in the statute of the International Tribunal, yet it was excluded. This is a very significant development because here we have a tribunal set up by the highest international body setting out a means of prosecuting people for the most heinous crimes known to civilization, and yet the death penalty is specifically excluded as an option.

The second issue involves three pending cases from Canada before the United Nations Human Rights Committee which deal with the issue of extradition. These three cases—the Kindler case,[15] the Ng case,[16] and the Cox case[17]—date from the time prior to when the United States had ratified the International Covenant on Civil and Political Rights. The Human Rights Committee is considering whether some issues raised by the death penalty are in fact in breach of Article 6 of the Covenant as they would be imposed in the United States, since these people are to be extradited to the United States or have been already. They are addressing, among

---

...in effect, what the United States said at the time was, "We will be bound by the International Covenant on Civil and Political Rights except with respect to the death penalty. Leave us alone on the death penalty. Don't ever hold us accountable for the death penalty before an international tribunal."

---

other things, the issue of the death-row phenomenon and the issue of the racist and discriminatory application of the death penalty.

The third issue concerns the United States' ratification of the International Covenant on Civil and Political Rights. The United States ratified the Covenant last year.[18] It came into force for the United States in September of 1992. But at the time of its ratification, the United States made a reservation to Article 6, which deals with the right to life, and to Article 7, which deals with the protection against torture.[19] These were death penalty reservations; and, in effect, what the United States said at the time was, "We will be bound by the International Covenant on Civil and Political Rights except with respect to the death penalty. Leave us alone on the death penalty. Don't ever hold us accountable for the death penalty before an international tribunal."

Now, the process of reservation is well recognized in international human rights law; and it is a very useful and helpful technique because it permits states to ratify human rights treaties even when they cannot be held completely accountable on some details or specific points before the international community. But international law makes it very clear that a reservation must not be incompatible with the object and purpose of a human rights treaty or any treaty, for that matter. In June, Sweden made an opposition to the U.S. reservation, insisting it is incompatible with the object and purpose of the Covenant.[20] And so the question arises, is the United States' reservation to the death penalty with respect to the International Covenant on Civil and Political Rights compatible with the object and purpose of that treaty? I submit that the authorities in international law, including the judgments of the Inter-American Court of Human Rights,[21] are quite clear: it is not. In other words, the United States' reservation is illegal, is contrary to international law. And this means, as a consequence, that the United States is bound by Article 6 and 7 of the International Covenant on Civil and Political Rights as a result of making this illegal reservation.

It also means that as of November 2, 1992—since which date the U.S. has executed five juvenile offenders—the United States has breached the International Covenant on Civil and Political

Rights to which it is a party and to which it has been bound since September 8 of 1992.

NOTES

[1] William A. Schabas, *Abolition of the Death Penalty in International Law*, Cambridge: Grotius Publications Limited, 1993.

[2] Amnesty International, *The Death Penalty List Of Abolitionist and Retentionist Countries* (December 1993).

[3] Argentina, Australia, Austria, Bolivia, Brazil, Colombia, Costa Rica, Czech Republic, Denmark, Dominican Republic, Ecuador, El Savador, Finland, France, Germany, Haiti, Honduras, Hungary, Iceland, Ireland, Italy, Liechtenstein, Luxemborg, Malta, Mexico, Mozambique, Netherlands, New Zealand, Nicaragua, Norway, Panama, Paraguay, Peru, Portugal, Romania, San Marino, Slovak Republic, Spain, Sweden, Switzerland, Uruguay, Venezuala.

[4] *American Convention on Human Rights* (1979), 1144 U.N.T.S. 123 O.A.S.T.S. 36.

[5] *Protocol No. 6 to the Convention for the Protection of Human Rights and Freedoms Concerning the Abolition of the Death Penalty*, E.T.S. 114.

[6] *Soering v. United Kingdom*, Series A, Vol.161.

[7] *Second Optional Protocol to the International Covenant on Civil and Political Rights Aimed at Abolition of the Death Penalty*, G.A. Res. 44/128 (1990) 29 I.L.M. 1464.

[8] *Universal Declaration of Human Rights*, G.A. Res. 217 A (III) U.N. Doc. A/810.

[9] *United States Constitution*, Amendment V.

[10] *Convention for the Protection of Human Rights and Fundamental Freedoms* (1955) 213 U.N.T.S. 221, E.T.S. 5.

[11] *International Covenant on Civil and Political Rights*, (1976) 999 U.N.T.S. 171, Art. 6.

[12] *Ford v. Wainwright*, 477 U.S. 399, 106 S. Ct. 2595 (1986).

[13] Note, supra, note 10, section 6.

[14] Statute of the International Tribunal, S.C. Res. 827 (1993).

[15] *Kindler v. Canada* (No. 470/1991) This case was dismissed in November, 1993: U.N. Doc. CCPR/C/48/D/470/1991.

[16] *Ng v. Canada* (No. 469/1991) In January, 1994, the Human Rights Committee concluded that execution in the gas chamber constituted inhuman treatment, and is a violation of Article 7 of the Covenant: U.N. Doc. CCPR/C/49/D/469/1991.

[17] *Cox v. Canada* (No. 486/1992) This case, judged admissible ((1992)13 HRLJ 352) is still pending.

[18] Amnesty International Report 1994, p.348.

[19] Multilateral Treaties, Reservations, Understandings, and Declarations, deposited with the Secretary General, status of December 31, 1992, st/leg/ser.e/11, page 132.

[20] Since September 1993, another 10 European states have formulated objections to the U.S. reservations.

[21] *Inter-American Court of Human Rights; Restrictions to the Death Penalty* (Art.s 4 sec.2 and 4 sec. 4 *American Convention on Human Rights*) Advisory Opinion O.C.-3/83 of September 8, 1983, Series A, No. 3, H.R.L.J. 352, 70 I.L.R. 449.

ABDOL KARIM LAHIDJI

IRAN AND THE DEATH PENALTY

I AM AN IRANIAN LAWYER living in France in exile. Here is a brief history of executions in Iran from 1988 to 1992.

■ *1988* and *1989:* More than 1200 political prisoners, of whom many had been sentenced to imprisonment, were executed in Iran. At least 142 people were executed for crimes of common law, such as murder, rape, and drug trafficking. Numerous executions took place in public and were announced in the official press.

After the uprising of the National Liberation Army, the amnesty of political prisoners became the object of strong attack in the Iranian press. The papers upheld that former political prisoners had participated in this uprising. They were said to be part of a group of 3000 prisoners who, after "fines" and "apologies," had benefitted from an amnesty on the ninth anniversary of the revolution. Executions were reported in every region of Iran, and many people who may have participated in the uprising of July 1988 were among the victims.

Some political prisoners were tried and condemned by tribunals that did not respect international norms guaranteeing fair trials. The accused were not allowed the assistance of lawyers or witnesses. The condemnations were often elicited under torture during extended periods of secret detention.

In July, Morteza Eshraqi, the Tehran Revolutionary Prosecutor,

ABDOL KARIM LAHIDJI A lawyer in private practice, earned his doctorate from the University of Tehran. Founder and Secretary of the Society of Iranian Lawyers, and Founder and Vice President of the Iranian Human Rights Society, Mr. Lahidji is also President of the Iranian Society for Human Rights (in Exile in Paris) which he founded in 1983.

announced that the death penalty would, from then on, be automatic for anyone found in possession of more than 30 grams of heroin or more than five kilograms of opium. Drug traffickers and murderers are often hanged in public, sometimes after being flogged. Four people were stoned to death for moral crimes. A death sentence was passed on a 16-year-old, found guilty of murder. A 17-year-old, convicted of rape, was hanged in public.[1]

■ *1989:* More than 1500 executions for common law crimes, of which more than 1000 were for drug trafficking, were announced in the official press. More than 40 people were executed by stoning. It is possible that political prisoners were among those executed for drug trafficking. It has been established that at least 2000 prisoners were executed between August of 1988 and January of 1989, but the number is probably much higher.

Multiple executions took place frequently, at times up to 80 victims were named in a single day in several towns. More than 250 executions were announced between January and the end of May for murder, rape, armed robbery, and prostitution. Thousands of people attended public stonings (43 cases), and the public even participated directly in certain cases. Twelve women and three men were stoned during one session in the soccer stadium in Bushehr.[2]

■ *1990:* More than 750 executions for common law crimes were announced in the official press. Numerous executions took place after group trials. A certain number of objectors in exile seem to have been victims of executions without trials perpetrated by government agents. It has not been possible to establish the number of political executions; most of them took place in secret.

In May, a law was adopted that extended the death penalty to infractions such as profiteering, food speculation and food hoarding which were denounced as economic terrorism.[3]

I have suffered a lot from my departure from the country where I lived for 40 years, but I am very glad to live in a country today (France) where the death penalty has been abolished.

■ *1991:* At least 775 people were executed. Most were condemned for criminal offenses, essentially for drug trafficking. There were reports that among those executed were more than 60 political prisoners, including members of the Kurdish Democratic Party of Iran, but this could not be confirmed. During the month of October, many Baluchis (Naroui tribe), including children and elderly people, were arrested. At least 20 men were executed in public in Jahedan shortly after their arrest.[4]

■ *1992:* At least 330 people were executed, including several dozen political prisoners. Eight people were executed after demonstrations in Shiraz, Arak, and Mashhad in April and May, after group trials during the days that followed their arrests. Forty-eight Baluchis, mostly from the Naroui tribe, were also executed, many of them hanged in public.

Dr. Ali Mozaffarian, one of the leaders of the Sunni community, was executed in August, having been charged with spying for the United States and Iraq, and also accused of adultery and homosexuality. Bahman Samandari, a member of a well-known Bahai family, was secretly executed in prison.[5]

As you can see, in these five years, not only did the number of executions not decrease, but most of the Iranians executed were political prisoners. And the Iranian government used the execution system for political reasons. Thousands of political prisoners have been executed under that pretext. I am speaking about a country where the rule of law is not respected. When the public participates in a stoning, that means that the social cohesion of the country disappears.

I have suffered a lot from my departure from the country where I lived for 40 years, but I am very glad to live in a country today (France) where the death penalty has been abolished.

NOTES

[1] *Amnesty International Report* 1989, pp.254-257.
[2] *Amnesty International Report* 1990, pp.122-125.
[3] *Amnesty International Report* 1991, pp.119-122.
[4] *Amnesty International Report* 1992, pp.144-146.
[5] *Amnesty International Report* 1993, pp.160-163.

DAVID MATAS

THE DEATH PENALTY AS A VIOLATION OF INTERNATIONAL HUMAN RIGHTS NORMS

THERE ARE basically two sets of international standards that relate to the death penalty. There are, on the one hand, optional standards to which states can accede. These are treaties which states can sign that commit them to abolishing the death penalty.

There are, on the other hand, the basic human rights that are essential to human dignity. They are universal, indivisible and non-derogable. They are not optional standards. They are fundamental minimum standards, *jus cogens*, binding on all states by virtue of their membership in the community of nations. Many of these standards relate to the infliction of the death penalty.

If we look at these two sets of standards, keeping the death penalty in mind, superficially it may seem that abolition of the death penalty is an optional standard. At international law, for those who have opted into this standard, the imposition of the death penalty is a violation of international law.[1] For those who have opted out, there are violations in the manner in which the death penalty can be imposed. But the death penalty simpliciter is not itself a violation of international law. Or so it seems.

The case of the United States is a test case. The U.S. violates the international standards which restrict the manner in which the

DAVID MATAS Human rights and refugee immigration lawyer in private practice in Winnipeg, Manitoba, Canada. Coordinator of the legal network of Amnesty International, Canadian Section, English-Speaking Branch. Co-chair of Canadian Helsinki Watch Group. President of Canadian Council for Refugees. Lecturer at University of Manitoba. Author of several books, including the forthcoming *No More: The Struggle Against Human Rights Violations*.

death penalty can be imposed. The case of the United States shows that it is impossible for the death penalty to be imposed in a manner which respects basic fundamental international human rights standards.

The United States is one of the oldest, largest, and strongest democracies in the world. The U.S. had a Bill of Rights in its constitution at a time when the very concept was foreign to many countries of the world. The symbol of the United States abroad is the Statue of Liberty, a symbol of human rights. The legal system of the U.S. is viewed abroad as a paragon of fairness, one that the emerging democracies around the world attempt to emulate, and to which all legal systems look for guidance and inspiration. And yet, in the U.S., not only is there the death penalty, there is a death penalty imposed in a manner that violates virtually all the relevant fundamental international standards.

To talk of a death penalty that is not cruel and unusual is an oxymoron, a self contradiction. The proof is the United States of America.

It is not merely that the death penalty will at some time in the future become a violation of international human rights law—when every state signs the Sixth Protocol to the European Convention on Human Rights,[2] or the Second Optional Protocol to the International Covenant on Civil and Political Rights,[3] or the Protocol to the American Convention on Human Rights to Abolish the Death Penalty[4]—the death penalty right now is a violation of basic, fundamental non-derogable international human rights law binding on all states. The death penalty by its very nature is arbitrary, discriminatory, racist. The death penalty will always and everywhere lead to the execution of innocent persons. Once a state has the death penalty, it will also end up with a nonfunctional clemency process. To talk of a death penalty that is not cruel and unusual is an oxymoron, a self contradiction. The proof is the United States of America.

It is not unfair to the death penalty to judge it by its workings in the U.S. If the U.S. cannot get it right, no state can. If the U.S.

cannot inflict the death penalty except in violation of basic human rights standards, it cannot be done. In one sense, the case is proved too well. The evidence is horrifying. There is the execution of the innocent,[5] of children,[6] of those with mental retardation,[7] of those who are mentally ill.[8] The horrors of the U.S. death penalty system are so many, so widespread, that one reaction has to be, surely it can be done better than that. The accused could be better represented. Jurors could be more fairly selected. Judges and prosecutors could be more ethical, more accountable. The clemency process could be made to work.

It is easy to think of an ideal world where the death penalty would work better than it is working now in the U.S. But in an ideal world there would be no crime, no murder, no need for criminal courts, and no call for the death penalty.

We cannot even say that the U.S. is the death penalty at its worst. The workings of the death penalty in Iran show widespread executions for crimes that do not involve killing;[9] with its use of stoning as a means of execution; with convictions based on testimony extracted through torture. The death penalty could in theory be operated better than it is in the U.S. In practice it can be and is run elsewhere in a far worse way.

Countries in Europe, before they abolished the death penalty, ran it far better than the U.S. One may ask, Why cannot the U.S. do it like that? To pose that question would be to ignore the linkage between the protection of legal rights in those countries and the abolition of the death penalty. The death penalty can survive only in a culture that is insensitive to human rights violations in the legal system. Once a country gets the death penalty right, the animus that leads to the death penalty disintegrates.

It is said that the faults of the U.S. legal system are not unique to death penalty crimes. In one sense, that is true. Yet in another sense, these faults are particularly acute in death penalty cases. An innocent person who is convicted and sentenced to prison may later be exonerated and released. But there is no forum for exoneration of the dead. Resurrection of the dead, executed in error, is beyond human powers. Exculpatory evidence that is suppressed by the prosecution may later surface and lead to a new trial. But when the prisoner is dead, the effort to release the suppressed evidence also dies. No legal system is infallible. Infallibility is beyond human powers. Given the imperfections of humanity, no matter how hard we try to overcome them, the response has to be not to impose the death penalty.

The abuses of the U.S. justice system are not just unfortunate accompanying incidents to the death penalty. In many cases they are caused by the death penalty, by the urge, the rush to execute. A death penalty process that respects human rights norms is a contradiction in terms. The death penalty process generates abuses in any justice system. If the death penalty is a violation of fundamental human rights, it is unacceptable to attack only its manifestations and not the violation itself.

Abolition of the death penalty is an evolving human rights norm. Abolition was foreseen by the Universal Declaration of Human Rights as early as 1948.[10] It was anticipated when Article 6 of the International Covenant on Civil and Political Rights was negotiated in 1957.[11] By the year 2000, the majority of states in the world will be abolitionist in law. Many of the states that are retentionist today in theory execute in practice not at all or extremely rarely. The countries that execute prisoners are fewer all the time. The countries that execute juveniles are a handful, with the U.S., in terms of numbers known to have been executed, in the lead. Abolition of the death penalty recently generated an optional protocol to the International Covenant on Civil and Political Rights—the only human rights norm that has done so. At some point, the abolition of the death penalty will emerge as an international human rights norm. I suggest that time has come.

One piece of evidence is the Charter of the ex-Yugoslav war crimes tribunal approved a few months ago.[12] The United Nations refused to impose the death penalty for the worst crimes imaginable, including genocide.

But the ultimate piece of evidence is the United States of America. The horrors we see in the U.S. death penalty system ultimately are not just U.S. horrors. They are death penalty horrors.

Based on the U.S. experience, I conclude:

1. International human rights law says the state must not execute arbitrarily. The death penalty is arbitrary. It represents a denial of fundamental justice and substantial due process. In 1972 the U.S. Supreme Court, in *Furman v. Georgia*,[13] struck down the death penalty because it was arbitrary. Various states of the U.S. have tried to devise a system that conforms to the Supreme Court guidelines on avoiding arbitrariness. These efforts have all failed.

The system today is as arbitrary as it was when the death penalty was struck down as unconstitutional. The imposition of the death penalty has more to do with time and place and money—that is, where the crime was committed, when it was committed, and whether the accused could afford a proper defense—than with the nature of the crime. The U.S. Supreme Court has lost interest in judging the arbitrariness of the system, as the case of *McCleskey*[14] shows. But that does not mean we should have no interest in it.

2. The death penalty is racist. In a sense, this is just one aspect of arbitrariness. Arbitrary does not just mean random. It also means imposition of the death penalty for reasons that have nothing to do with the crime. Another set of international standards come into play here, standards that guarantee equality. The death penalty violates these standards as well.

The death penalty is legal lynching of blacks by whites. The response of the U.S. courts is not that this racism is not happening, but that the courts do not care whether it is happening or not. The U.S. criminal justice system, of which the death penalty is an integral part, is a form of social control of its black community. Although there are many white victims of the death penalty, if there were no racism in the U.S., there would be no death penalty. The death penalty is a continuation of the tyranny of slavery in another form. It is no coincidence that the death penalty in the U.S. is strongest in the former slave states, the states of the old Confederacy.

3. A death penalty trial is an unfair trial. One component of a fair trial is the right to counsel. The right to counsel means the right to effective assistance of counsel.

If there is one fault that is pre-eminent among all the miscarriages of justice in the U.S. death penalty system, it is the inadequacy of defense counsel. Yet, that inadequacy is unavoidable.

Accused persons who are potentially subject to the death penalty are almost uniformly indigent. Their lawyers are assigned by courts and paid extremely poorly, in some states only about $1600 per case. The estimated counsel time needed to defend adequately an accused person subject to the death penalty can range from 800 to 1000 hours. Consequently, counsel who have done an adequate job have found themselves earning approximately two dollars an hour.

The number of lawyers willing to work those hours, for that fee, is small. For the bulk of those potentially subject to the death penalty, the only way to ensure an effective defense is to pay defense counsel a reasonable remuneration.

That would mean that for each case where an accused is potentially subject to the death penalty, the court-appointed or legal aid system would have to allow for defense counsel a sum that no legal aid system, even in the wealthy U.S., will ever be able to afford. The result is that a death penalty system is a system doomed to be tainted by ineffective counsel.

4. One human rights standard in the application of the death penalty is that innocent persons are not to be executed. The evidence of the execution of innocents is incontrovertible. Given the irrevocability of the death penalty and the fallibility of human judgment, the numbers of innocent individuals convicted and executed will continue to mount. There are people on death row today for whom there is compelling evidence of innocence.

5. Non-derogable international human rights standards require where there is a death penalty, it must not lead to the execution of children, or of those who are unable to appreciate the nature of the crime or punishment.

The U.S. death penalty allows for the execution of juveniles. It is this aspect of the death penalty in the U.S. that in theory appears most severable from the rest. However, to succumb to this view is to ignore the reality of the death penalty. Human rights violations, like human rights themselves, are indivisible. In the U.S., the linkage between the death penalty and the execution of juveniles is inextricable.

6. The death penalty leads to the execution of the mentally ill and of those with mental retardation. The death penalty is the imposition of power on the powerless. And the most powerless and least able to defend themselves are those with mental disabilities. Despite the obvious inappropriateness of subjecting such people to the death penalty, they become one of its prime targets.

7. Another international standard is that, where there is the death penalty, there must be effective parole or clemency procedures. The death penalty leads to an ineffective clemency process. Again, in theory it might seem possible to have both the death penalty and a functioning clemency system. But with an effective clemency process, virtually no one would be executed. In every death penalty case the arguments for mercy are compelling. But with large scale clemency, the appetite for state killing that generated the demand for the death penalty could never be satiated. To satisfy the appetite for state killing represented by the death penalty, the clemency process has to be undermined.

8. The prohibition against cruel and unusual treatment is both an international standard and a U.S. standard. The death penalty is cruel, inhuman and degrading. The death penalty is cruel and unusual. The European Court of Human Rights, in the case of Soering,[15] has already found that the wait for execution on death row is cruel, inhuman and degrading. The U.S. inflicts lethal chemicals and gas, firing squad, electrocution, and hanging. They are all cruel, inhuman and degrading.

9. The death penalty is akin to torture. There is the case of Jesse Tafero[16] whose head caught on fire in a botched execution; and the case of another prisoner whose execution in the electric chair took nineteen minutes.[17] If a person is hooked up to electricity or poisoned for interrogation, but allowed to survive, it is clearly torture. How can killing a person by the same method be anything less?

10. The death penalty is a violation of the respect for life. That proposition may seem obvious. Historically, the death penalty was seen as an exception to the respect for life. It is time to conclude that the exception no longer has any international status or validity. Respect for life should prevail, without exception.

NOTES

[1] Amnesty International, "United States of America, Open letter to the President on the Death Penalty," January 14, 1994, p.3.

[2] *Protocol No. 6 to the Convention for the Protection of Human Rights and Fundamental Freedoms Concerning the Abolition of the Death Penalty*, E.T.S. 114.

[3] *Second Optional Protocol to the International Covenant on Civil and Political Rights Aimed at the Abolition of the Death Penalty*, G.A. Res. 44/128 (1990) 29 I.L.M. 1464.

[4] *American Convention on Human Rights*(1979) 1144 U.N.T.S. 123 O.A.S.T.S. 36.

[5] For examples such as James Adams, executed in Florida in 1984, see Hugo Adam Bedau and Michael L. Radelet, "Miscarriages of Justice in Potentially Capital Cases," *Stanford Law Review*, Vol.40, No.1 (November 1987), p.73.

[6] *Rumbaugh v. Texas*, 629 S.W.2d 747.

[7] *Dunkins v. Alabama*, 489 So.2d 603.

[8] *Louisiana v. Prejean*, 379 So.2d 240, cert. denied, 499 U.S. 891, 66 L.Ed. 119, 101 S.Ct. 253 (1980).

[9] Amnesty International, *Death Penalty News*, March 1994.

[10] *Universal Declaration of Human Rights*, G.A. Res. 217 A(III) U.N. Doc. A/810.

[11] *International Covenant on Civil and Political Rights*, (1976) 999 U.N.T.S. 171, Art. 6.

[12] Statute of the International Tribunal, S.C. Res. 827 (1993).

[13] 408 U.S. 238 (1972).

[14] *McCleskey v. Kemp*, 481 U.S. 279 (1987).

[15] *Soering v. U.K.*, Series A, Vol. 161.

[16] Michael L. Radelet, "Post-Furman Botched Executions," April 15, 1992, p.2.

[17] Ibid.

NICOLO AMATO

ABOLITION OF THE DEATH PENALTY BY THE YEAR 2000

RECENTLY, thanks to the determined efforts of the International League for the Abolition of the Death Penalty by the Year 2000, the Italian Chamber of Deputies abolished the death penalty from the Military Code in wartime and in peacetime, and Italy joined the ranks of those European countries which have already abolished capital punishment from their legal systems. This may appear to be merely a formal act, but we believe form and substance are one in legal matters and that the death penalty must be abolished *de jure* and *de facto*, and that its being abolished must constitute the first step in the creation of a new individual right. We will continue campaigning until the right of every human being not to be killed following a sentence or judicial measure, even if issued by law, is affirmed in the fundamental texts of individual states and of the international community.

We must first create a Europe without the death penalty, in order to arrive at an important confrontation between the European and American democratic model, to establish an international "consuetude" confirming that the state has no right to dispose of the life of any individual, whatever crime he or she may be guilty of, and to make this supreme right the basis of the entire international human rights system.

NICOLO AMATO is a member of the Transnational Radical Party and the International League for the Abolition of the Death Penalty by the year 2000. He is also a member of the Promoting Committee of the International League which held its first world Congress in December 1993 in the European parliament in Brussels.

We will continue campaigning until the right of every human being not to be killed following a sentence or judicial measure, even if issued by law, is affirmed in the fundamental texts of individual states and of the international community.

The International League, of which I am a member, is composed of parliamentarians from all over the globe, Nobel Prize winners, celebrities from the worlds of culture and science, human rights activists, and ordinary citizens, all of whom have committed themselves to giving top priority to abolishing the death penalty from the laws of every single country before the symbolic date of the year 2000. The International League is organizing a worldwide parliamentary campaign which aims to present, in logical and progressive sequence, abolitionist motions, documents, and other texts in parliaments throughout the world so that jointly inspired bills with a common aim may be presented on the same day, at the same time, in as many parliaments as possible. This project is supported through the mobilization of public opinion and the media.

Working in the same direction, we made every effort to ensure that the Italian proposal for setting up an international court to judge war crimes in the former Yugoslavia excluded the possibility of the application of the death penalty. The project was accepted by the United Nations Security Council with the passing of Resolution No. 827 on the 25th of May, 1993, and will now constitute, if it becomes a permanent International Court, a fundamental part of supra-international law to which all countries must conform.

How can any one of the 37 American states that practice capital punishment legitimately inflict the death penalty when the international community, of which the United States is a member (in the same way that it is a member of the Security Council which passed Resolution 827), excludes the death sentence not only for very serious war crimes, but also for genocide? It is an absurd contradiction, but one we hope will eventually produce positive results. There is no doubt that the international role played by the

United States makes it a crucial front on which to conduct our abolitionist campaign, and the more than 2,800 people who have been condemned to death and are waiting to be executed on American death rows are a precise indication of the problem we are up against.

The decisions that will be taken regarding the life or death of each of these individuals will affirm or negate the values on which a tolerant, modern democracy, capable of facing and of overcoming contradictions, must be founded—values which will also sustain this new democracy. We propose to start by imposing a moratorium on all executions immediately in order to gain time to modify international and national laws accordingly. This moratorium must last for a minimum of three to five years and, at the same time, the United States must ratify the International Covenant on Civil and Political Rights (ICCPR).[1] We intend to present, in as many parliaments as possible, motions inviting governments to object to the reservations made by the United States at the moment of signature concerning those clauses in the convention which provide for strict limitations on the executions of minors, pregnant women, and mentally handicapped persons. This would constitute the first major confrontation between abolitionist countries and Clinton's America.

We firmly believe that the United States is capable of abolishing the death penalty in the same way that it abolished slavery, by upholding a new law which supplanted traditions and constitutions, economic and social systems, and deeply rooted beliefs and prejudices. The first movement to abolish slavery was founded in England in 1787, and seven years later the convention abolished slavery in the French colonies. While enslavement was widely condemned in Europe between 1800 and 1875, Islamized regions in Africa continued their slave trading. This inhuman practice was abolished in the northern United States at the beginning of 19th century; nevertheless, in the South, a few white families still owned as many as three million slaves in 1860. Five years later, the 13th Amendment to the U.S. Constitution abolished slavery once and for all. We can abolish the death penalty as we abolished slavery and prohibited torture, simply by reforming the penal system and recognizing the threshold of inviolability of individuals' rights, which exists precisely because it is confirmed by law. Also, in a penal system it is necessary to establish an irreducible human value which will make us a single human family, as Boutros Boutros-Ghali so wisely commented at the United Nations World Conference on Human Rights in Vienna.

NOTES

[1] The United States ratified the ICCPR in September 1992.

RAMSEY CLARK

A LAND OF VIOLENCE

THE UNITED STATES is a land of violence. We are a country that will slaughter a quarter of a million people in Iraq and celebrate it with a ticker tape parade. We are a very materialistic people. We love things. But we glorify the power of violence and ignore its pity. We are a people that manufacture a machine called the "Trident 2" nuclear submarine that can launch 24 missiles simultaneously while submerged. In deference to disarmament we have cut back the number of warheads each missile can carry from 17 to 8, which means that the Trident 2 can launch simultaneously 192 independently targeted nuclear warheads towards centers of population and incinerate a million people each, nearly 200 million people, perhaps causing nuclear winter, rendering earth, beautiful earth, as lifeless as the moon. You have to come to grips with the mentality that has enabled this society to construct such a monstrous machine that in human terms is unthinkable. How could it ever be used?

RAMSEY CLARK Private law practice, New York City and Washington, D.C., 1969 to present; actively engaged in the practice of law in the fields of the death penalty, international law, constitutional law, criminal justice, human rights, civil rights, First Amendment, and other subject areas; 1961-1968: nominated assistant Attorney General of the United States by President John F. Kennedy, served to 1965; nominated Deputy Attorney General by President Lyndon B. Johnson, served to 1967; nominated Attorney General, served to January 20, 1969; was the first Attorney General to propose abolition of the death penalty. Teacher: legal seminars on civil rights planning, law as an effective instrument for social change: Howard University School of Law, Brooklyn Law School; Author, among other books: *The Fire This Time: U.S. War Crimes in the Gulf*, 1992, Thunders Mouth.

Our land is awash with physically battered women and brutalized children, armed robbery, assaults and murder. In the late 1960's, the U.S. Department of Justice took its first and only stand in history against the death penalty. At that time we found that 95 percent of the people convicted of murder in the first degree in a test state had been themselves victims of childhood abuse.

The role of racism in executions reeks absolutely. It is undeniable. It's the same racism that directs so much of our militarism and our foreign policy. We didn't begin keeping statistics on what we call criminal justice executions, which is an oxymoron, until the early 1930's. From that time until some thirty years later when executions for rape were prohibited by the Supreme Court of the United States as constituting for that crime cruel and unusual punishment, 89 plus percent of all the people executed for rape were African-American.[1] I defy any analysis to explain that fact in any terms other than racial hatred. We have yet to discover a single case where the victim of the rape for which a man was executed was an African-American. All have been white Americans.

Our death penalty isn't spread generously across the land; it's focused intensely in special places and among certain types of people. I come from Texas. It's a land we took from Mexico by force. It's a land that Mexico recognized they would lose before it was taken. I can show you the "Matamoros Eagle" edition for December 16 (Beethoven's birthday), 1835, in which they say that the United States is going to take Texas from Mexico because its fertile coastal planes could feed all of their people.

There were no executions in the United States from 1968 until 1977. 1968 was the last year of the great emotional outpouring that began in the 40's and 50's in the noblest quest of the American people in my time, our Civil Rights movement. It gave birth to the movement to end poverty, to achieve equality for all, including women, and to control violence. The first really powerful feminist movement in the United States after World War II came out of this same effort. It was a movement against violence and for the control of guns. And 1968, the year that saw the assassination of Martin Luther King, our great prophet of nonviolent social change, and Robert Kennedy, the year of the worst race riots in the history of the United States, with more than a hundred cities afflicted with racial riots caused by social injustice, that was the first year in our history in which there were no executions.

Since 1977 Texas has executed more people than 45 other states combined. Joe Jernigan, executed in Texas on August 5, 1993, was denied an order by the courts that he was entitled to a hearing before the Texas Board of Parole on commutation, a constitutional right in Texas implemented by statutes from the Legislature elected by the people. No hearing was granted. The law has failed to face the death penalty. The consequences are tragic.

There is a judicial crisis of unprecedented dimension in our United States as a direct result of the death penalty. There can be no question about it. It exceeds the crisis that followed the "Dred Scott" decision because that case, while evading and aggravating the problems of slavery, could not have ended the irreconcilable conflict between slave and free states.[2] The courts have the power and the duty to end the crisis caused by the death penalty once and for all under the constitution, if they choose to. Their failure to do so has damaged the courts, judicial administration, constitutional rights and respect for the rule of law.

The death penalty crisis is greater than that which followed *Brown v. Board of Education*, which discovered what every schoolchild and parent ought to have known—that segregated educational facilities are inherently unequal.[3] Why did we put an African-American child in a shabby school with no books or pencils or paper? Racism, because we wanted him to be ignorant, just as the slave codes prohibited teaching slaves how to read and write. But the courts addressed the problem of racial segregation by public schools, however inadequately, and now Legislatures and school administrators bear the major responsibility for ending this wrong. The death penalty, while authorized by law, cannot be evoked by the courts. Every case must come before the judiciary. It is the greatest judicial crisis we have had. The courts can't stand it. They will not face these cases. The Board of Parole in Texas won't give hearings. The judiciary won't consider the effect the death penalty is

For 50 years our greatest jurists have told us we have to choose. Every society has to choose. If we want truth and justice, we cannot have the death penalty. If we want power and violence, the death penalty will be a principal instrument.

having on it, on justice, on the country and reverence for life. They are acting in a totally irrational way.

For 50 years our greatest jurists have told us we have to choose. Every society has to choose. If we want truth and justice, we cannot have the death penalty. If we want power and violence, the death penalty will be a principal instrument.

Danny Harris was executed in Texas on July 30, 1993. He was 17 when the crime for which he was convicted occurred. That crime resulted in a death. Whether Danny Harris was responsible remains uncertain. His brother had been executed for the same crime on July 1, 1993. There have been 62 executions in Texas since 1977, far more than any other state. Nearly 400 people are on Texas' death row.[4] It is imperative that we act boldly with all the international support we can get to end the death penalty.

When working on the Gary Gilmore case in '76 and '77, I remember the Governor of Utah stating he understood all these 'do-gooders' in the United States telling him he shouldn't let Gary Gilmore be executed by a firing squad. It didn't bother him much. But he was proud of his country, and all the criticism coming from foreign nations was hard for him to accept because he thought we were number one, we were the civilized country, we were the teacher, we were the decent and gentle people.

We all can learn a simple lesson I learned from a man I represented and loved as powerfully as I can love my grandchildren or my sister or my mother. His name was Carlos Santana. He was born in the Dominican Republic and raised in abject poverty. I went into the execution chamber with Carlos on March 23, 1993, at about 2:10 A.M. We had talked earlier for several hours and he was calm and thoughtful. Now, we had just received the decision from the

Supreme Court of the United States denying a stay of his execution. As I walked in, he was strapped on a gurney, very much as if on a cross with both arms extended. He had five wide bands across him, holding him down. He was asked whether he had anything to say by two men in crisp suits which must have just been returned from the cleaners. Carlos lifted his head and looked at us. There were five friends in the room. He looked at each face. Carlos was prolific in his outpourings of poetry and letters and love. He wrote legal briefs for other people on death row. He was enormously respected by the staff of the penitentiary, who couldn't look him in the face, and by the inmates who knew him. After looking at each of us, he said: "Love is the answer, not hatred. I love you all." Within two minutes Carlos Santana, a man who had never hurt anyone, left his wife a widow and his two children orphans, by the deliberate act of the state. God help us.

We need action to end the death penalty in the United States to save the soul of this nation.

NOTES

[1] *Crime in America*, Ramsey Clark, Simon & Schuster, 1970, p.313.
[2] *Dred Scott v. Stanford*, 60 U.S. 393 (1857).
[3] *Brown v. Board of Education*, 347 U.S. 483 (1954).
[4] As of October 5, 1994, 82 people had been executed in Texas since 1977, NAACP Legal Defense and Educational Fund, Inc., *Execution Update*, October 5, 1994; As of July 20, 1994, there were 385 people on death row in Texas, NAACP Legal Defense and Educational Fund, Inc., *Death Row, U.S.A.* (Summer 1994).

DIANN YVONNE RUST-TIERNEY

THE UNITED STATES GOVERNMENT AND THE DEATH PENALTY

I AM THE DIRECTOR of the Capital Punishment Project for the American Civil Liberties Union. The American Civil Liberties Union's work against the death penalty focuses on three areas of public education: educational forums, legal advocacy through our affiliates, and legislative advocacy, primarily with the U.S. Congress. In our view, the death penalty is a fundamental violation of due process and equal protection. We believe it is also a fundamental violation of human rights.[1]

When the Supreme Court ruled in *Furman v. Georgia*[2] that then existing death penalty statutes violated the Constitution because they were administered in an arbitrary and capricious way, it not only invalidated state death penalty statutes, but federal death penalty statutes as well. Unlike the states, however, the federal government has not been able to revive the death penalty wholesale. It has been enacted narrowly for only a few offenses. Currently under federal law the death penalty is available for: peacetime espionage by people subject to the Uniform Code of Military Justice,[3] drug-related murders under the 1988 Drug Abuse Act,[4] and murder under the U.S. Military Code in general.[5]

The struggle at the federal level is whether the death penalty

DIANN YVONNE RUST-TIERNEY Director, American Civil Liberties Union, Capital Punishment Project. Vice-Chair, National Coalition to Abolish the Death Penalty. Co-wrote, co-directed, and co-produced educational video, *Double Justice: Race and Capital Punishment* (1993). Testified on death penalty legislation and related issues before the House Judiciary Subcommittee, the Senate Judiciary Committee, and the U.S. Sentencing Commission.

In our view the death penalty is a fundamental violation of due process and equal protection. We believe it is also a fundamental violation of human rights.

will be revived broadly, as it is in the states, whether the death penalty will be available for first degree murder generally where there is federal jurisdiction, and whether it will be available for specific federal crimes, such as treason, espionage, and mail bombing.

With the exception of the Administration in which former Attorney General Ramsey Clark served, the position of the United States Government has been foursquare in support of the death penalty. In recent years that advocacy has become more extreme, culminating in the Bush Administration's position that the death penalty was the appropriate punishment for over 50 offenses.[6] The Bush Administration's tilt for death departs from our Constitutional law which holds that the death penalty is to be applied only narrowly.[7] It also violates international human rights standards which require the death penalty to be limited, if it is to be available at all.[8]

Today the United States is poised to expand the death penalty to more than 60 crimes.[9] The Clinton Administration has made it well known that it supports the death penalty and intends to pick up where its predecessor left off. We may be able to persuade this Administration to be somewhat more careful in the procedures it would propose for imposing the death penalty, but the desire to broadly expand that penalty remains. This proposed expansion of the death penalty at the federal level presents yet another opportunity to widen the injustices we see at the state level.

The 1988 Drug Abuse Act has been in existence for only a short time, yet we see the same disparities in racial discrimination that we see at the state level. To date there have been 37 prosecutions for so-called drug-related murders, and all but four of the people currently prosecuted under that statute have been African-American or other people of color.[10]

Another disturbing innovation we have seen in the prosecution of these cases is the use of "gang" trials. Rather than trying people as individual defendants, we see numbers of young African-American males tried as groups.[11] Such trials raise numerous questions of due process. They also bear an eerie similarity to former death-penalty prosecutions in South Africa.[12]

It is important to note that what the federal government does serves as a model to the states. To the extent the death penalty is federally expanded, it serves as a model for the states to do the same.

One of the most disturbing aspects of the federal government's aggressive support for the death penalty has been the pressure to expand the availability of the death penalty to non-homicidal crimes, particularly in the area of drug kingpins and drug trafficking.[13] As drug offenses in the United States are of great concern, it has become politically expedient to propose the death penalty for drug kingpins, notwithstanding the fact that the Supreme Court long ago said the death penalty should be available only for homicides.[14]

In the Bush Administration, lawyers worked to craft legal arguments to support the death penalty for non-homicidal crimes.[15] It is bad enough that the federal government would take this great step away from the mandates of the Constitution. The prospect that the states may follow makes this result all the more chilling.

The broad scope of the death penalty raises the risk of discrimination. Particularly when you move outside the sharp line drawn by a homicide, the potential for the kind of harms we have seen at the state level is increased.

...this debate is not about a difference of opinion concerning domestic law enforcement but about a fundamental human rights violation.

We have been able, at the federal level, to get some protection for people with mental retardation and other mental disabilities, and to exclude the death penalty for people who were under 18 at the time of their crime.[16] However, with each press for expansion of the death penalty, we expect those protections to be undermined. In fact, when they were proposed during the last Congress,[17] we came very close to having 17-year-olds executed. We also came close to having people with disabilities other than mental retardation executed.

The voice of the international community is very important in this debate. Even anti-death penalty members of Congress do not fully appreciate the death penalty as an international human rights violation. The American people in general certainly have little appreciation of that fact. From time to time I must remind even myself that this debate is not about a difference of opinion concerning domestic law enforcement but about a fundamental human rights violation.

Some people think this is just a part of our criminal justice system, that we have had it a long time, and so it is something we do. Others do not know or understand the full weight and implications of the international experience of those countries that have rejected the death penalty.[18] The judgment of the international community is that as a human society we are beyond this punishment.[19] It is crucial that we understand and express the human rights dimension of this struggle. It adds a level of respect and high ground to a political landscape which is otherwise the scene of public fear, anger, and frustration.

NOTES

[1] See for example, *International Covenant on Civil and Political Rights*, Article 6; see also *Human Rights Violations in the United States*, prepared by the ACLU, December 1993, pp. 93-106.

[2] 408 U.S. 238 (1972).

[3] 10 U.S.C. sec 918.

[4] 21 U.S.C. Sec 848(1).

[5] 10 U.S.C. Sec 918.

[6] *Bush Administration's Comment on The Comprehensive Violent Crime Control Act of 1991*, p.2; see also testimony of William Barr before the House Subcommittee on Crime, Committee on the Judiciary, March 14, 1990, pp.318-81.

[7] See supra note 2; see also *Gregg v. Georgia*, 428 U.S. 153 (1976).

[8] See supra note 1.

[9] See for example, H.R. 3355 and H.R. 4092, the Omnibus Crime bills from the 103rd Congress. The Federal Crime Bill was passed by the U.S. Congress on August 25, 1994.

[10] *Racial Disparities in Federal Death Penalty Prosecutions: 1988-1994*. Prepared by the House Subcommittee on Civil and Constitutional Rights, Committee on the Judiciary, March 1994, p.3.

[11] *U.S. Richard Tipton, et. al.* 4th Circuit case #93-400567, 9, & 10 (appeal pending).

[12] Bruck, David, "On Death Row in Pretoria Central," *The New Republic*, July 13 & 20, 1987, pp.18-25.

[13] See Title II of H.R. 3355 and Title VII of H.R. 4092 (103rd Congress); see also *Comparison*

of the Senate and House Crime Bills on Key Civil Liberties Issues, prepared by the ACLU, May 12, 1994, pp.4-5.

[14] *Coker v. Georgia*, 433 U.S. 584 (1977).

[15] *Hearings before the Subcommittee on Crime of the Committee on the Judiciary* (House of Representatives). March 14, 1990. Testimony of William Barr, Assistant Attorney General, Office of Legal Counsel, U.S. Department of Justice, pp.318-364.

[16] 21 U.S.C. Sec 848 (1).

[17] See supra note 6, pp.2-22.

[18] *The Death Penalty in Wartime: Arguments for Abolition*, prepared by Amnesty International, January 1994, pp.1-2.

[19] Ibid.; see also Article 6 of the *International Covenant on Civil and Political Rights*.

PAUL HOFFMAN

INTERIM MEASURES

THE UNITED STATES should take interim measures on the road to the abolition of the death penalty. How can interim measures do, when all that really is applicable is rage? How can interim measures do, when only complete abolition will do?

Perhaps if the people of the United States—and then their elective representatives—were forced to examine the same evidence that the Amnesty International Commission of Inquiry into the Death Penalty in the United States has examined (and very few people in the United States have heard that evidence)—maybe they would decide that the death penalty is something they can not accept.

Maybe if the people of the U.S. knew that the rest of the world was different, that the rest of the world had different standards, that the rest of the world understood that the death penalty was inconsistent with fundamental principles of humanity and justice, maybe then they would change their minds and we would not have the death penalty.

PAUL L. HOFFMAN established his own law firm on March 1, 1994. The firm concentrates in constitutional, civil rights and international human rights litigation. From 1984-1994, Mr. Hoffman was Legal Director, ACLU Foundation of Southern California, Los Angeles, where he specialized in cases involving First Amendment rights, AIDS discrimination, criminal justice and the death penalty. In March 1991 he testified before the House Subcommittee on Civil and Constitutional Rights about police abuse in Los Angeles. He is currently an Adjunct Professor at both the University of Southern California Law Center and Loyola University College of Law and the author of numerous Law Review articles.

I ask for complete abolition always, but, at a minimum, we need steps towards abolition. Let me suggest five.

We know that juvenile offenders, children who are convicted of killing before reaching their 18th birthday, are executed in the United States. There could not be a clearer example of American law at variance with international law, with basic principles of humanity that are unquestioned even by representatives of the United States. Yet, the Senate of the United States, in the Bush Administration, found it necessary when the U.S. ratified the International Covenant on Civil and Political Rights to have a reservation to even this basic principle that children convicted of killing should not be executed.[1]

The Clinton Administration needs to know; the Senate needs to know; the people of the United States need to know that we can't execute children. This is not something that can be accepted in this country.

Similarly, there are clear international standards prohibiting the execution of those with mental retardation and the mentally ill. The U.N. Economic and Social Council has passed these resolutions.[2] The world has accepted them. The United States at international meetings has not rejected them. The U.S. should not accept the execution of the mentally ill or of those with mental retardation. The people of the United States must speak truth to power and tell those in power that this cannot be accepted, and it must stop immediately. Even if the people of the United States continue their embrace with the death penalty, they cannot execute the mentally ill and those with mental retardation, even by their own standards of morality.

Race: there is overwhelming evidence about the implications of race and the death penalty in the United States. The evidence cannot be ignored. It is a reality. The United States Supreme Court found a way to avoid that reality. It said: "We understand there's racism, and that's a terrible shame, but unless you can find the one racist that's responsible, unless you can pin responsibility in the courtroom on one person that has intentionally caused this death sentence based on race, then we can't do anything about it."[3]

That is not acceptable, because the people of the U.S. have a responsibility under international law, and even under the U.S. Constitution, to make sure that no one is put to death because of racial discrimination. There has been the Racial Justice Act before the U.S. Congress for years, and it at least seeks to create standards, procedures, that would eliminate racism in the implementation of the death penalty. At a minimum, that must be done.

The U.S. must try to eliminate racism in the death penalty. It cannot hide behind legal doctrine. The U.S. must implement international standards prohibiting racial and ethnic discrimination. The burden must be on the state to show that there is no racial discrimination; the burden should not be on the poor person on death row or on their lawyers to show that there is discrimination.

The way that the death penalty system operates in the U.S. cannot be called due process, by any humane, reasonable definition.

The fourth proposed interim measure is in the area of fair procedures and due process. Americans claim that this is a country based on those principles. Those principles are incorporated and enshrined in the United States Constitution, and they are accepted in universally accepted international standards, including the International Covenant that the United States has just ratified. The United States accepted those principles in the International Covenant without reservation (except in regard to the execution of juveniles).[4]

The way that the death penalty system operates in the U.S. cannot be called due process, by any humane, reasonable definition. You cannot give a person a court-appointed lawyer hired by the state, give him/her a few dollars to handle his/her first case with no time for investigation, no time for consideration, barely enough time to talk to the person she or he is representing, and call that due process. But once the trial is over, then in the appellate process there are doctrines to shield this scandalous reality from meaningful examination. One is that the judgment of the trial court must be final. Second, there may have been a procedural default at the trial. If the trial lawyer

The world has a goal, a principle of humanity of ultimate abolition, and it has been accepted for decades. That is the way of the future; that is what human rights require.

didn't raise an objection to an error at trial, then the appellate lawyer cannot complain about it on appeal. Third, new evidence doesn't matter; if the person is innocent, that's a shame, we'll do it better the next time around. That's what the *Herrera* case says.[5] That can't be accepted.

There are international standards that require due process, and due process must come. Now people are meeting in corridors and closed rooms and smoke-filled rooms and talking about how to dismantle what is left of *habeas corpus* in the U.S., so that the death penalty machine can run without any interference, without any delay. That must be stopped. People should have every chance to show their innocence, to show that there should be no execution.

Finally, there's the question of the proliferation of new death penalties. The world has a goal, a principle of humanity of ultimate abolition, and it has been accepted for decades. That is the way of the future; that is what human rights require. The United States has made a mockery of that principle. The United States Congress cannot wait to add new death penalties. The Congress looks for new categories of people to get the death penalty for killing. The death penalty grows like Topsy. In the States, there are new death penalties all the time.

The United States cannot be allowed to thumb its nose in the face of the entire world community by doing that. It must be held accountable; it must accept the principle of ultimate abolition. There must be a moratorium not only on new death penalties but also on the execution of people already on death row.

Give the people of this country time to hear what the Amnesty International Inquiry into the Death Penalty in the United States heard. Have this moratorium, have no more victims, have no more sacrifices on the altar of politics and expedience while this debate goes forward. The American people must have that debate. I have confidence that if they hear what the Commission heard, the people of the U.S., not the people they send to Washington or to State Houses in Texas or Georgia, but the people of the U.S. will reject this punishment.

NOTES

[1] Multilateral Treaties, Reservations, Understandings, and Declarations, deposited with the Secretary General, status of December 31, 1992, st/leg/ser.e/11, page 132.

[2] *Safeguards Guaranteeing Protection of the Rights of Those Facing the Death Penalty*, adopted by the UN Economic and Social Council in resolution 1984/50 at its 1984 Spring session on 25 May 1984 and endorsed by the UN General Assembly in resolution 39/118, adopted without a vote on 14 December 1984.

[3] *McCleskey v. Kemp*, 481 U.S. 279 (1987).

[4] *International Covenant on Civil and Political Rights*, (1976), 999 U.N.T.S. 171, ratified by the United States in 1992.

[5] *Herrera v. Collins*, 113 S.Ct. 853, 122 L.Ed2/203, (1993).

SAM REESE SHEPPARD

IN THE BELLY OF THE DEATH PENALTY BEAST

"IT'S MIGHTY, mighty strange that the best of friends have got to part. You know last night I got me a letter. What do you reckon it read? You know last night I got me a letter, what do you reckon it read? It said, 'You better come on home, Sam boy, because the gal you love is dead.'" The words of Son House, Mississippi blues singer.

At the age of seven I suffered the trauma of the murder of my pregnant mother. She died on the night of July 4, 1954, in the bedroom next to where I slept in our home in Bay Village, Ohio. Five and one half months later, the State of Ohio asked a jury to condemn my father to death. First the trauma and then the terrorism, from violent death to the threat of more violent death.

My father did not murder my mother. He was an innocent man. But the fourth estate was looking for a strong rope and a low limb. The major metropolitan area of the City of Cleveland, Ohio, became embroiled in a hysteria of lynch mob proportion. Vigilante justice and lynching are a documented fact of the past, part of the

SAM REESE SHEPPARD is Vice-Co-Chair of Murder Victims Families for Reconciliation and serves on the Board of Directors of the National Coalition to Abolish the Death Penalty, and Massachusetts Citizens Against the Death Penalty. Today a public speaker on the human rights violations of the death penalty, children's rights, the crisis of violence in the USA, the need for real prison reform and victim/survivor concerns, Mr. Sheppard lost his mother to murder when he was seven years old. Within months the state of Ohio had convicted his father (Dr. Sam H. Sheppard) for the crime and was demanding the death penalty. Sentenced to life imprisonment, Dr. Sheppard ultimately was able to establish through blood stain patterns that he was not his wife's killer, and he was acquitted.

collective memory of American consciousness, and, I fear, all too real a memory for many of us who are involved in the work of ridding the world of human execution.

Research points to the fact that a crowd can take on a dimension of its own. It can deteriorate into madness, panic, and riot. Many parliaments in the world have recognized this danger and ruled out the option of death as a punishment. Democracy is vexed to vote against vengeance in the face of her own fear on this issue of violence.

In the summer of 1954, the Sheppard case literally saved a metropolitan newspaper from bankruptcy and allowed it to carry on business for another 20 years. At least five books about the case and, so I'm told, numerous newspaper articles and TV reports, persist to this day, close to 40 years later. A made-for-TV movie appeared in 1976. A popular television series called "The Fugitive," whose story line was based loosely on the Sheppard case, aired in the mid-1960's. In 1993, a major Hollywood movie, based on this series, opened in theaters across America.

The trauma of the murder, the subsequent terrorism of the threat of the death penalty and the following years of prison visitation and further court actions blew our family apart. My mother died by murder. My father served ten years in prison for a crime he did not commit. Later exonerated, he could not survive in a society that vilified him.

What do I inherit from all this economic activity taking place over the memory of my dead loved ones? Little but a call to do another interview or make comments upon the ongoing case in which we search for the murderer of my mother, and the relation of this case to the second generation fiction of Hollywood movie production.

The trauma of the murder, the subsequent terrorism of the threat of the death penalty and the following years of prison visitation and further court actions blew our family apart. My mother died by murder. My father served ten years in prison for a crime he did not commit. Later exonerated, he could not survive in a society that vilified him. My paternal grandmother committed suicide. My paternal grandfather died of massive gastric ulcers soon after the first courtroom battle. My maternal grandfather committed suicide. At least three members of the family drank themselves to death, and one died of drugs. The remaining family members live apart throughout the United States. Most are unable or unwilling to speak of this tragedy in their lives.

I know absolutely that if my father had been executed, as threatened, when I was a child, with that event coming so closely upon the loss of my mother, I would not be alive today. The horror on top of the terror and trauma would have torn me apart.

I grew up in a state of shock. I am lucky to be alive. I have been told by experts that people like me who've had my experience do not survive. But some children in this country live today in this terrible limbo, waiting for the execution of a loved one, innocent or guilty, and mothers await the killings of their sons.

The children on both sides of the victim/offender equation suffer horribly and in a similar manner. The ego boundaries of young lives fluctuate to blame these deaths, this violence, upon themselves. I know that misplaced guilt. It is the guilt of an innocent seven-year-old child who awoke one morning to the sudden loss of his whole world, the murder of his mother nearby and his father to face the threat of the death penalty soon thereafter.

I know people, some of the walking wounded, who feel the constant pain and shock and frustration of being caught in the mad loss of their loved one. And others, equally wounded, who live with the imminent threat of execution for their loved ones. Loved ones of the victim, loved ones of the offender. I see a serious need for the development of social and psychological programs and social responsibility for the survivors of these violent deaths. Sometimes whole communities suffer the trauma of these incidents.

One day after talking with a very pained woman who cried out for the reinstatement of the death penalty, the interviewer turned to the little girl who stood by her mother's side. She asked the lit-

I urge Amnesty International to extend further human rights research into the belly of the beast, the abyss of the prison system in this country, that if allowed to proliferate unchecked, will incarcerate one half of the population of the United States by the year 2058.

tle girl what she thought of all this. The child thought a moment then said, "I don't know, but Mama's teaching me to hate so good."

The death penalty in the United States today is a hate crime. It teaches vengeance, hatred and revenge are acceptable values to be cultivated and lived by in our society. We must change this ethic for the good of civilization. I recently talked with some grade school children in their classroom about the death penalty. The children expected a guest, but they did not know who was to visit. As we stepped into the room, one little boy said, "Arnold Schwarzenegger."

This points to a problem in American society. This man lives the successful life of the American dream. This man has the money, the women, the prestige and fame, but this man in his movie career to this point has killed over 150 people in the fantasy land of the cinema. These values grow within the hearts of our children, the values of payback, revenge and violence. The pain and hurt in this country show themselves in every city, they cry out in our newspapers and on our TV screens.

July 4th, 1994, is the fortieth anniversary of my mother's death. Twenty-three years ago my father died from the abuses of the prison system and subsequent public vilification in this country. I grew up with a father in a maximum security prison. My dad went to the hole on occasion because that was the only place he could be alone. In that hole he stood naked in the dark between two doors because he did not have the space to sit down or stand up in the United States of America. I grew up with a jump frisk, the threat of a strip search, and exposure to the violent homophobia that the prisons in this country cultivate.

I urge Amnesty International to extend further human rights research into the belly of the beast, the abyss of the prison system in this country, that if allowed to proliferate unchecked, will incarcerate one half of the population of the United States by the year 2058.

The Sheppard case lives on as an unsolved case, as a landmark case in U.S. jurisprudence and the constitutional question of fair trial versus free speech and free press in this country. The economic system still pumps out the publicity, the books, the articles, the TV shows and the films. The death penalty sells. Television and newspaper profits jump dramatically when a high-profile case appears. Politicians and lawyers profit in notoriety, power and career-advancement.

We must stop the abuse of the freedoms of speech and press in the name of profit and free enterprise. We must stop buying violence and its aftermath. Viable alternatives to the death penalty do work, such as meaningful prison sentencing, prison industries, and restitution payments to the victims' families. We must free democracy and civilization from the danger of our own fear, exhibited by execution. We must respond to the acts of horrific violence upon our own kind. We must lead our world from the love of violence into acceptance of reconciliation and peace-making. Let us stop teaching the next generations to "hate so good."

BILL PELKE

THE SEEDS OF COMPASSION

I HAD THE OPPORTUNITY on July 11, 1986, to sit in on a death penalty case. The facts of the case were these: a 78-year-old Bible teacher had been murdered; there were four young girls involved in the crime. Three of the girls already had been sentenced for their parts in the murder. They received 25, 35, and 60 years respectively. The fourth girl remained to be sentenced.

I was there as the prosecution sought, in fact demanded, the death penalty. I was there as the prosecution presented its witnesses, including a psychologist, who said that the defendant was a sociopath, and a family member of the deceased, who had found the body and testified that it would be a travesty of justice not to order the death penalty.

I was there as the defense presented witnesses asking for the mercy of the court in its sentencing. Several family members of the defendant begged the judge and justice system for mercy. I was there as the defendant made a statement asking for forgiveness from the victim's family and mercy from the court.

Judge James Kimbro delivered his verdict. He stated that when he had graduated from law school in 1959, there was one thing he knew for sure, and that was that he was opposed to the death

---

BILL PELKE A Vietnam veteran, is the Founding Board Member of Murder Victims Families for Reconciliation (MVFR), and the originator of the idea for the Journey of Hope, two-week marches through different U.S. states which bring people from all over the world together to speak out for abolition. Mr. Pelke has worked at Bethlehem Steel for 28 years and is Amnesty International's Death Penalty Abolition Coordinator for the state of Indiana.

penalty. He related how in that era in this country the majority of people were opposed to the death penalty. He related how he had seen that pendulum swing to the other direction where now the majority of the people in the United States favor the death penalty. He stated that he "hoped that some day the American public would have their fill of the blood that had been shed through the death penalty and that the pendulum would swing back in the other direction."[1]

He then went on to pronounce that due to the laws of the State of Indiana, he had no other choice, and he sentenced Paula Cooper to death. Paula Cooper was 15 years old at the time of the crime.

I believe that it is lucky for a man to know what his mission is in life. It was four months after this trial that I received mine. At the time I was having some personal problems, mainly a relationship that was breaking up. I was very depressed and indulged in self-pity. I was basically looking to my God and saying, "Why my life? Why am I even here?"

I did this for a period of time, and then I began to think about someone who had a whole lot more problems than I did. I pictured an image of Paula Cooper, the young girl I saw sentenced to death. I pictured her slumped against the side of her cell with tears rolling down her cheeks, moaning, "What have I done? What have I done?" She was very much alone. Her parents were not even at the hearing when she was sentenced to death.

I recalled from the trial, as the Judge began to deliver his sentence, an old man crying and wailing, "They're going to kill my baby. They're going to kill my baby." I recalled how Paula's grandfather was escorted from the courtroom by the bailiff, and I recalled the tears running down the old man's cheeks as he was led past me.

It was at that point I pictured an image of my grandmother.

...he "hoped that some day the American public would have their fill of the blood that had been shed through the death penalty and that the pendulum would swing back in the other direction."

There were tears flowing down my grandmother's cheeks. There was no doubt in my mind that they were tears of love and compassion for this young girl and her family and what they were going through.

My grandmother, Ruth Pelke, had been murdered by this girl. Yet, I was convinced that my grandmother would have been appalled by the fact that Paula Cooper was on death row and that her family would be involved in this situation. My grandmother was a Bible teacher, my grandmother believed in forgiveness, and I was convinced that my grandmother wanted someone in our family to have the same compassion that she would have had for Paula and her family. It seemed to fall on my shoulders.

Having absolutely no love and compassion for this girl, I was convinced nevertheless that I must try to generate some. My grandmother's tears dictated to me to find a way. So, in tears, I begged God to give me compassion for Paula Cooper and her family. That prayer was answered immediately.

It was at that point that my life became dedicated to spreading the seeds of love and compassion. The experiencing of that compassion was the greatest blessing of my life. It brought love and forgiveness for the girl who had so brutally murdered my grandmother.

Ruth Pelke had been stabbed 33 times with a 12-inch butcher knife. It was a very, very heinous crime. Yet, that gift of love and compassion was so beautiful and so important in my life that I have spent the last six and a half years working for love, compassion and reconciliation.

Paula Cooper's case became well-known. When Paula received the death sentence, it was reported in newspapers throughout the European community. Italy ran a series of stories about Paula's situation, and there was great interest in her case.

I received a telephone call from an Italian journalist about four or five months after my plea of love and compassion for Paula. The journalist said she was coming to the United States to do a story on Paula. She had called the local paper that had covered Paula's trial and asked for good sources to interview. The person at the newspaper had recommended Paula's grandfather, Paula's attorney,

The death penalty is the tip of the iceberg. It is what we can see plainly. We can see that there are over 2800 people, human beings, on death row in the United States and that this country wants to kill these people. But, our problems are deeper than that. The answer is love and compassion for humanity.

and also a grandson of the victim who had written an article in the paper talking about love and forgiveness.

The Italian journalist said to me, "We don't picture Americans as being very forgiving people, and we would like to be able to talk to you when we come to Indiana." I was more than happy to comply because one thing had been very clear to me. Since the gift of love and compassion had been granted, I no longer wanted Paula to die, and I wanted to do everything I could to help her.

When the interview took place, I was informed that over 40,000 Italians, mostly school children, had signed petitions to be sent to Indiana requesting that Paula Cooper be taken off death row. A group called "Don't Kill" had also been formed on Paula's behalf.

This group was tremendously important to me because in northwest Indiana there was little or no support for Paula Cooper. When people found out that I was supporting Paula and did not want her to die, they thought I was crazy. This was true of friends, family and co-workers. When I heard there were 40,000 people who had signed petitions, I was definitely overwhelmed with joy and gratitude.

As a result of the articles written when the journalist went back to Italy, I had an opportunity to appear on an Italian television program that was doing a story about Paula. The Italians' fascination with Paula's case continued to grow.

When it became known that I was going to Italy on behalf of Paula Cooper, the American media also became very interested in what I was doing. Numerous requests for interviews came in. I was thankful for the opportunity to go to Italy because I wanted to thank those 40,000 people who had signed the petitions and to deliver a message of love and compassion.

Many events took place in Paula's case. Over three million Italians ultimately signed petitions to have Paula Cooper taken off death row. The Pope, through regulations and chain of command, contacted the Governor of Indiana and requested a pardon for Paula.

The international media cast a shadow of embarrassment over the State of Indiana when it was made known that state law allowed ten-year-old children to get a death sentence. Indiana immediately passed a bill raising the execution age limit to 16 (at the time of the crime).

When Paula Cooper's appeal before the Indiana Supreme Court took place, Paula was taken off death row. Her sentence was reduced by the Court to 60 years in prison. The Court attributed part of the reason for its decision to the fact that Indiana had raised its age limit to sixteen. That legislation specifically had provided that the change in law not affect Paula Cooper, but the Court said to execute Paula under the old law, would be unfair.

Because of the pressure brought by the international community, Paula Cooper's life was saved. That pressure got her off death row. The international community has a tremendous power that can be added to our efforts for abolition here in the United States.

We held an event last month in the Midwest called the Journey of Hope. People gathered from around the world for this event and it was truly a journey of hope. The Journey was hosted by an organization called Murder Victims Families For Reconciliation (MVFR), a group of people who have had someone in their family murdered and yet, united, stand opposed to the death penalty. With a loud and powerful voice, MVFR says vengeance is not the answer. The Journey of Hope was a great success.

The death penalty is the tip of the iceberg. It is what we can see plainly. We can see that there are over 2800 people, human beings, on death row in the United States and that this country wants to kill these people. But, our problems are deeper than that. The answer is love and compassion for humanity.

NOTES

[1] *State of Indiana v. Paula Cooper*, July 11, 1986.

WILLIAM J. BOWERS

POPULAR SUPPORT FOR THE DEATH PENALTY: MISTAKEN BELIEFS

I AM Principal Research Scientist in Criminal Justice at Boston's Northeastern University. I have conducted research on capital punishment in the United States since 1972, and published two books, *Executions in America* (1974) and *Legal Homicide* (1984),[1] that report the results of my earlier work.

Since 1990, Margaret Vandiver[2] and I have conducted research on the death penalty attitudes of ordinary citizens, their elected legislators, and persons who have served as capital jurors in the United States.[3] My own research on capital punishment began with a study of racial bias, which became *Executions in America*, in some 5,000 state-imposed executions in the United States between 1864 and 1967. This study showed systematic racial disparities in the use of capital punishment, consistent with the U.S. Supreme Court's 1972 *Furman v. Georgia*[4] ruling that the death penalty violated the Eighth Amendment of the U.S. Constitution because it was being imposed in an arbitrary and discriminatory manner under existing statutes. I returned to the questions of arbitrariness and racial bias in capital punishment after the Supreme Court's 1976

WILLIAM J. BOWERS Principal Research Scientist, College of Criminal Justice, Northeastern University. Co-Author of: *Legal Homicide: Death as Punishment in America, 1864-1982*; *Execution in America*, 1974. On editorial boards of: *Criminology, Journal of Criminal Law and Criminology*; *Law and Society Review*; *Journal of Research on Crime and Delinquency*; *Law and Human Behavior*. Testified: as an expert witness in 26 capital cases (1976-1991); also before the Subcommittee on Criminal Justice, Committee of the Judiciary, U.S. House of Representatives, concerning death penalty legislation (June 4, 1986).

Gregg v. Georgia[5] decision permitted a return to capital punishment under "guided discretion" capital statutes, supposed by the Court to remedy such arbitrariness and discrimination. My initial work with Glenn Pierce on the imposition of the death penalty under newly enacted statutes in Florida, Georgia, Ohio and Texas (and other, more refined later investigations), clearly demonstrated that the new laws did not remove the racial bias declared unconstitutional in *Furman*.[6]

Confronted with the strongest of this evidence in the 1987 *McCleskey v. Kemp* case,[7] the Supreme Court, by a one vote 5-4 margin, made a profound retreat from its stance in *Furman*. It ruled that even strong system-wide evidence of racial disparities would not protect defendants from the punishment of death.[8] A key element, in the majority's view, was that the system-wide statistical evidence did not impeach the exercise of sentencing discretion by individual capital jurors. The Court declared that such statistical evidence does not reveal how jurors in capital cases actually make their sentencing decision. This faith of the Court in capital jurors' exercise of discretion provided the impetus for our present study of jurors who served on capital cases in 13 states across the country.

Our research on the attitudes of citizens and legislators has its roots in a series of surveys initiated by Amnesty International USA in Florida (1985 and 1986) and followed in Georgia, Nebraska, Oklahoma, New York, Virginia, California and Kentucky.[9] These Amnesty surveys yielded a remarkable revelation about the shallowness of death penalty support as expressed in the polls. Specifically, the Amnesty studies revealed that although public opinion polls show that three out of four Americans say they favor the death penalty, this expressed support drops to one in four when people are asked: "If this state could impose a sentence of life without parole and require offenders to work in prison for money that would go to the families of victims, would you prefer this as an alternative to the death penalty?" In every survey that asked this question, or one very much like it, most people said "yes" they would prefer the alternative over the death penalty.

In New York we found that 71 percent of our respondents said they "favored" capital punishment, but only 19 percent said they would stick with the death penalty if the alternative was life without parole plus restitution. In Nebraska, where 80 percent initially "favored" the death penalty, only 26 percent would stick with it if given this alternative. These 52 and 54 percentage point drops in death penalty support are a strong indication that people are merely giving lip service to the death penalty in the public opinion polls—cited by the Supreme Court in its *Gregg* decision as indicating that Americans want capital punishment.

This, after all, is the essence of arbitrariness... the public recognizes and acknowledges the truth of what made the Supreme Court declare the death penalty unconstitutional in *Furman*.

In our New York and Nebraska studies, we followed up this evidence of the shallowness of such support with death-penalty-specific questions that revealed considerable ambivalence in public attitudes toward the death penalty. We showed that this ambivalence was a major source of the readiness to abandon the death penalty in favor of an alternative. Eighty-three percent in New York and 84 percent in Nebraska said, "The death penalty is too arbitrary because some people are executed while others serve prison terms for the very same crimes." This, after all, is the essence of arbitrariness. In effect, the public recognizes and acknowledges the truth of what made the Supreme Court declare the death penalty unconstitutional in *Furman*.

More than this, we found that people place a greater emphasis on compensatory and restorative aspects than on punitive treatment. The citizens of New York and Nebraska put top priority on punishments that provided for compensation or restitution to the victim, or family of the victim. Thus, 93 to 95 percent in each state said, "If we really cared about crime victims, we would make offenders work to pay for the losses and injuries their victims have suffered," and "A good way to make criminals feel responsible for their crimes would be to have them work in prison to pay for the harm they have done." Thus, the alternative of a life sentence with a restitution requirement is more consistent than the death penalty with the public's top punishment priorities.

Evidence of the illusory character of expressed death penalty support is not new. Earlier studies have revealed the "symbolic" nature of death penalty attitudes, the fact that expressed support is abstract, ideological, irrational and nonempirical, that it erodes when confronted with the particulars of crimes and defendants, with responsibility for its application, and with information about the realities of capital punishment. Recent surveys have identified alternative punishments for convicted murderers that cause most people to abandon the death penalty in favor of an alternative, particularly one that eliminates the possibility of parole and requires the convicted offender to work in prison for earnings that would go to murder victims' families. Our research in New York and Nebraska has:

1. shown that a majority preference for such a death penalty alternative holds in widely divergent settings and even among those who express strong support for capital punishment;

2. identified general punishment priorities and specific death penalty attitudes that support the preference for such an alternative; and

3. found that the widespread preference for a death penalty alternative is altogether unappreciated by lawmakers in New York State.

Even in the most crime-ridden urban areas and even among people who say they "strongly" favor capital punishment, we found majority preference for an alternative to the death penalty. People in high-crime urban districts are as receptive to a death penalty alternative that denies parole and requires work for restitution to victims' families as are statewide samples with much less experience with or concern about serious crime. In all of these settings, majorities of those who initially expressed "strong" support for capital punishment on the standard polling question nevertheless preferred an alternative. This raises a fundamental question about the meaning of such expressions of death-penalty support. Indeed, the

...the fact that it is neither information nor arguments against the death penalty but the prospect of a harsh and perhaps more meaningful alternative that erodes even strong death-penalty support suggests that the death penalty is a hollow symbol to most who say they favor it.

fact that it is neither information nor arguments against the death penalty but the prospect of a harsh and perhaps more meaningful alternative that erodes even strong death-penalty support suggests that the death penalty is a hollow symbol to most who say they favor it.

Our work suggests that public support for capital punishment is an illusion that has become a self-perpetuating political myth. The expression of such support is a tenuous reflection of a culturally-induced but unstable desire for punitiveness as a response to crime and other problems of social order. It holds appeal as an expressive symbol, not as a policy preference. It has become a self-perpetuating political myth because pollsters have rested their interpretations on a single misleading indicator of death-penalty support; because the media have reported this interpretation without reservations, qualifications or caveats; and because politicians have used death penalty advocacy to capitalize on the public's fear of crime.

Margaret Vandiver and I asked capital jurors, as well as the public, about the arbitrariness of capital punishment. In the three states—California, Florida and South Carolina—where our juror interviews have been completed, we found that 76, 83 and 86 percent, respectively, of those who actually decided whether the defendant should live or die felt: "The death penalty is too arbitrary because some people are executed while others go to prison for the same crime." Another question we put to jurors also reflects arbitrariness in their decision-making. We asked: "How long murderers not sentenced to death will serve in prison before being paroled or released back into society?" Across the board, public and jurors alike underestimated the punishments that would otherwise be imposed.[10] This mistaken impression obviously makes some people feel the death penalty is needed.

We learned in addition that jurors' decisions about whether or not to impose the death penalty may be a product of their misperceptions about the alternative presently available in their states. We can divide our jurors into those who served on juries that did and did not impose the death penalty. On both kinds of juries, jurors underestimated the time a convicted offender would serve before returning to society, but in each state, those on juries that imposed death sentences were *more wrong* in that they mistakenly thought the offender would be back in society sooner. So, the mistaken belief that the alternative punishment will be more lenient than it actually is in practice appears not only to prop up public support for capital punishment, but also to encourage jurors to impose death as punishment.

NOTES

[1] William J. Bowers, *Executions in America*, Lexington, MA: D.C. Heath, 1974; William J. Bowers, Glenn L. Pierce, and John F. McDevitt, *Legal Homicide: Death as Punishment in America, 1864-1982*, Boston, MA: Northeastern University Press, 1984.

[2] Margaret Vandiver is an Assistant Professor, Department of Criminology and Criminal Justice, Memphis State University.

[3] *Capital Jury Project* (National Science Foundation Grant 90-13252).

[4] 408 U.S. 238 (1972).

[5] 428 U.S. 153.

[6] William J. Bowers and Glenn Pierce, "Arbitrariness and Discrimination under Post-*Furman* Capital Statutes," *Crime and Delinquency* 26 (October 1980): 563. Reprinted as Chapter 7 of *Legal Homicide*.

[7] 481 U.S. 279.

[8] In a reversal of his position, Justice Lewis Powell, the fifth vote in the *McCleskey* decision, revealed in a recent biography, *Justice Lewis F. Powell, Jr.* by John C. Jeffries, Jr., Charles Scribner's Sons, New York, 1994, that he now believes his vote was incorrect.

[9] *An Analysis of Attitudes Toward Capital Punishment in Florida* (Washington, D.C.: Cambridge Survey Research, 1985); *An Analysis of Political Attitudes Toward the Death Penalty in the State of Florida: Executive Summary* (Washington, D.C.: Cambridge Survey Research, 1986); Thomas and Hutcheson, *Georgia Residents' Attitudes Toward the Death Penalty, the Disposition of Juvenile Offenders, and Related Issues* (Center for Public and Urban Research, College of Public and Urban Affairs, Georgia State University, 1986); Nebraska survey: Johnson and Booth (Bureau of Sociological Research, 1988); Grasmich and Bursik, *Attitudes of Oklahomans Toward the Death Penalty* (Center for the Study of Crime, Deliquency and Social Control, 1988); *New York Public Opinion Poll, The Death Penalty: An Executive Summary* (Cambridge Survey Research, 1989); Virginia survey (Commonwealth University Research Survey Center, 1989); Haney and Hurtado, *Californians' Attitudes about the Death Penalty: Results of a Statewide Survey* (Field Research Corporation, 1989); Vito and Kell, *Attitudes in the State of Kentucky on the Death Penalty* (Urban Research Institute, University of Louisville, 1989).

[10] Supra note 3.

MARGARET VANDIVER

CAPITAL JUROR INTERVIEWS

WHILE CONDUCTING jury interviews with Dr. William Bowers,[1] we found overwhelming misunderstandings of the law. Jurors who sit in capital cases and make life-and-death decisions do not understand the judges' instructions; they do not understand the requirements of the law.

Out of 49 jurors interviewed in North Carolina, only two were able to tell us properly what the legal requirements of mitigating testimony were. And in every instance where the jurors were mistaken, their mistake made a death sentence more likely. The misunderstandings are very deep. They run throughout the trial and the sentencing process.

Jurors find the experience of having to make life-and-death decisions to be excruciatingly painful and morally very difficult. To serve on a capital jury in this country, you must be in favor of the death penalty. We are not talking about opponents of the death penalty, we are talking about people who are selected to serve because they support the death penalty.

Here are a few quotes from jurors:

MARGARET VANDIVER Assistant Professor, Department of Criminology and Criminal Justice, Memphis State University. Author or co-author of: "The Quality of Mercy: Race and Clemency in Florida death penalty cases, 1924-1966," *University of Richmond Law Review* (forthcoming); "Coping with death: Families of the terminally ill, homicide victims, and condemned prisoners," pp.123-138 in M.L. Radelet (ed.) *Facing the Death Penalty: Essays on a Cruel and Unusual Punishment*, Philadelphia: Temple University Press, 1989; *Capital Punishment in America: An Annotated Bibliography*, New York and London: Garland Press, 1988.

> *"We were so upset after imposing death, we were still standing in the parking lot crying for about 30 minutes. Six months passed before I stopped thinking about it constantly.*
>
> *"I cried at the end when watching them walk the defendant's crying mother out of the courtroom. It was so difficult sentencing someone to death. I had the sense of killing someone."*
>
> *"My decision for the death penalty was very hard. It hurt me greatly that I had to make the decision on someone's life."*
>
> *"I had nightmares about other people who may be given death. I wanted the defendant to get the easiest form of death possible."*

One final quote from a juror in Virginia:

> *"Can I live with this if I give the man the death penalty? How will I feel when they are strapping this man down in the chair? How would I feel after they pronounce the man dead? Can I live with this? Will it work on my mind? Will it drive me crazy in the years to come?"*

Racial bias in the imposition of the death penalty in this country is rampant. I don't intend to paraphrase these quotes. These are the actual words of jurors as they were tape recorded in our interviews.

In a death case in Florida we asked the juror about feelings and impressions concerning the defendant, and were told:

> *"I was impressed from the trial that there are two definite lifestyles. The black community was entirely different from the way I was raised and the way we lived. The value of life—it's totally different." "The defendant had a lower value on life than I did."*

"Can I live with this if I give the man the death penalty? How will I feel when they are strapping this man down in the chair? How would I feel after they pronounce the man dead? Can I live with this? Will it work on my mind? Will it drive me crazy in the years to come?"

In a South Carolina case we asked the juror if the defendant reminded him of anyone:

> "*Yeah, about the hundred blacks, every field hand, all the blacks that I've known around here just about. Just typical.*"

In another Florida capital case, we asked for a description of the defendant:

> "*He was a professional black. He moaned about his problems and blamed them on a white society being against a black male — he should have blamed his problems on his own shortcomings.*"

In a Kentucky case this is what we were told about a defendant who had testified:

> "*No, he seemed pretty smart, you know, he put himself on the stand. I would say he was above average as far as that race is concerned.*"

In a North Carolina capital case we asked for a description of the defendant:

> "*Just a typical nigger.*"

When the same juror was asked if she found any difficulty answering questions during jury selection, she replied:

"If they had asked me if I was prejudiced, that would've been hard for me to answer."

"Did they ask?"

"No. But if they had, I would've had to say yes. Anybody that was born and raised in the South when I was born and raised in the South and says they're not prejudiced is a liar. I try very, very hard to get over it. Every time I get somewhere I meet a nigger. That's the way it is. And what difference between me and the others is I admit it. I mean, when I heard about this killing, I thought, 'Well, they're just wiping each other out again.' You know, if they'd been white people, I would've had a different attitude."

NOTES

[1] *Capital Jury Project* (National Science Foundation Grant 90-13252).

BARBARA FREY

INTERNATIONAL STANDARDS AND THE EXECUTION OF JUVENILE DEFENDANTS

WITHIN the international community there is strong consensus for abolishing the death penalty for defendants who are 18 or younger at the time of their crimes. Currently, more than 70 countries have included provisions within their laws stating that persons under 18 years of age may not be subjected to the sentence of death.[1]

Twelve other countries are presumed to have similar laws in place because of their accession to the International Covenant on Civil and Political Rights[2] or the American Convention on Human Rights.[3] Only a few governments besides the U.S. continue to execute juvenile offenders. Between 1985 and 1990, executions of juveniles are known to have been carried out in five countries: Iraq, Pakistan, Saudi Arabia, Yemen and the United States.[4] During the 1990's juveniles are known to have been executed in only three countries: Saudi Arabia, Yemen and the United States.[5]

Despite the international trend toward abolishing the practice of executing juveniles, the U.S. continues to have more juveniles on death row than any other country. Since the reinstatement of the death penalty after *Furman v. Georgia*,[6] 125 juvenile death sentences have been imposed on people between the ages of 15 and 17

BARBARA A. FREY Executive Director, Minnesota Advocates for Human Rights; Adjunct Professor in International Human Rights Law at University of Minnesota Law School. Active in diverse human rights issues internationally. Recipient of Minnesota State Bar Association, Civil Litigation Section, Advocacy Award (1993). Author and editor of human rights articles and reports.

at the time of the crime. (Of these imposed sentences, as of October 20, 1994, 41 remain in force in 13 U.S. states.[7])

In analyzing the situation of these youthful offenders, Amnesty International and other groups have documented that juveniles on death row have a disproportionate number of social and psychological problems, including unstable and abusive family backgrounds, drug and alcohol addiction at a very young age, mental illness and brain damage.[8] Unfortunately, this information does not always come out in court as evidence to prevent the imposition of the death penalty.

Children have a special status in international law, a status that is now enshrined in the Convention on the Rights of the Child,[9] adopted by the United Nations in November 1989. There are already 164 state parties to the convention. Article 37 of the convention provides that children under 18 convicted of crimes shall not be subject to capital punishment, life imprisonment, torture or cruel and inhuman punishment.

The sentiment reflected in the Convention is that every child deprived of liberty be treated in a manner which takes into account the needs of persons of his or her age. It calls for a variety of dispositions in criminal convictions that ensure children are dealt with in a manner appropriate to their well-being and proportionate to the circumstances of their offense. The Children's Convention has not even yet been signed by the United States, in large part because of its strong prohibition on juvenile executions. The actions of the U.S. are well out of the international mainstream on this issue.

The international community has consistently seen juveniles as less responsible for their actions than adults.[10] Because of their

---

...this apparent abandonment of hope for rehabilitation of juvenile offenders is inherent in the criminal justice system and seems to be the result of a distressingly high level of fear and cynicism among the American public, political leaders and court personnel.

---

youth, juveniles are viewed as more likely to rehabilitate than those who have reached the age of majority.[11] The imposition of the death penalty on persons who have not attained full physical or emotional maturity is recognized as inappropriate and inhumane, because it permanently denies the child any chance of rehabilitation or reform.[12]

Unfortunately, this apparent abandonment of hope for rehabilitation of juvenile offenders is inherent in the criminal justice system and seems to be the result of a distressingly high level of fear and cynicism among the American public, political leaders and court personnel. It is my feeling that extensive public education is needed to counterbalance that fear and restore a sense of morality to America's legal system with regard to its treatment of minors.

There is well-established international law prohibiting the execution of persons who are under 18 at the time of their offense.[13] Besides the Convention on the Rights of the Child, there are several treaties which forbid such executions, including the Fourth Geneva Convention,[14] which was adopted in 1949, and the International Covenant on Civil and Political Rights,[15] both of which have been ratified by the United States Government.

The American Convention on Human Rights,[16] which the U.S. has signed but not yet ratified, also prohibits the use of the death penalty on those under 18 at the time of the crime.[17] The first appearance of the prohibition of juvenile execution in an international agreement was Article 68, Paragraph 4, of the Fourth Geneva Convention. The Geneva Convention regulates behavior during wartime. The U.S. has signed and ratified this agreement without ever asserting any opposition to that article.[18]

The United States signed the International Covenant on Civil and Political rights in 1977 and ratified the treaty on June 8, 1992. This treaty, in Article 6(5), reads, "The sentence of death shall not be imposed for crimes committed by persons below 18 years of age."

U.S. ratification of the Civil and Political Covenant, however, carried the following reservation: "The U.S. reserves the right, subject to its Constitutional constraints, to impose capital punishment on any person other than a pregnant woman duly convicted under existing or future laws permitting the imposition of capital punishment, including such punishment for crimes committed by persons below 18 years of age."[19]

This reservation is attached to the U.S. ratification of the Civil and Political Covenant, despite serious questions raised by groups such as Amnesty International as to whether a reservation to a non-derogable right such as Article 6 can be valid.[20] I expect and hope that we will see this question put before the UN Human Rights Committee in the near future.

Our regional human rights treaty, the American Convention on Human Rights, which was signed by the United States in 1977, provides that capital punishment "shall not be imposed on persons who, at the time the crime was committed, were under 18 years of age or over 70 years of age."

While the U.S. has not ratified the American Convention, the Inter-American Commission on Human Rights has found that the American Declaration on the Rights and Duties of Man is binding on the U.S. as a member state of the OAS.[21] The American Declaration contains several general provisions that could be interpreted through customary international law to prohibit the execution of minors, including Article 1, "The Right to Life," Article 7, "Special Protection of Children," and Article 26, "No Cruel, Infamous or Unusual Treatment."[22]

In a 1987 case before the Inter-American Commission, the case of James Terry Roach and Jay Pinkerton, two minors who had already been executed in South Carolina and Texas respectively, the Commission held that the U.S. violated Articles 1 and 2 of the American Declaration because the federal government has left the issue of the juvenile death penalty to the discretion of state officials, resulting in "a patchwork scheme of legislation which makes the severity of the punishment dependent, not primarily on the nature of the crime committed, but on the location where it was committed."[23]

In dicta, the Commission found an emerging customary norm establishing 18 as the minimum age for the imposition of the death penalty, although it refrained from applying such a norm against the United States because of the proposed reservations of the U.S. Government to the American Convention.

While the Commission did for the first time find that the U.S. violated its international obligations through juvenile execution, its decision would have been much clearer and more influential within the United States if it had been based on customary international law and not on equal protection under the federal scheme.

The domestic law of the United States also recognizes that children have a lesser responsibility within the community than do adults.[24] We see this distinction in both the civil and the criminal law systems.

The U.S. practice of killing minors is abhorrent to the international community, violating both the letter and the spirit of the law.

The age of majority in 44 states is 18, while five states have set the age of majority at 19.[25] It is ironic that a person does not possess the legal capacity to enter into a contract until the age of 18, yet eight states set a minimum age of 16 or 17 for conviction and sentencing in a capital case.[26] Similarly, while the U.S. Supreme Court has twice made reference to international standards and practices when faced with the issue of juvenile executions, to date, it has failed to prohibit the execution of all offenders younger than eighteen as a matter of Federal constitutional law.[27]

The U.S. juvenile court system expressly prohibits the imposition of the death penalty upon juvenile offenders. The commonly held belief within the juvenile court system is that children should be treated and rehabilitated. The focus of the court, therefore, is on the child's condition, not his or her guilt.

However, juvenile courts rarely will maintain jurisdiction in cases involving extremely serious crimes, such as rape or murder. These cases are seen as too serious to be dealt with within the juvenile court system, and the child is transferred to a criminal court for determination of guilt and subsequent sentencing under guidelines used for adults. A juvenile may receive a sentence of death within the criminal court.[28]

In states that have set a minimum age below which the death penalty cannot be imposed, juveniles can still be transferred to adult criminal courts to receive their punishment, but they cannot receive the death penalty under any circumstance. Out of the 36 states within the U.S. that currently have the death penalty,[29] 25 states have laws allowing juvenile offenders to be executed within the adult criminal court system.[30]

In conclusion, the weight of international law clearly supports the abolition of juvenile executions. The U.S. practice of killing minors is abhorrent to the international community, violating both the letter and the spirit of the law. Children are to be given special status and an opportunity for rehabilitation.

It is not enough to present juries with evidence of the offender's youth or special circumstances at sentencing hearings. We must take these cases out of the realm of the subjective and sensational, and rejoin the international community by finding new and more humane ways to deal with the societal problem of juvenile violence.

NOTES

1 Amnesty International, *United States of America: The Death Penalty and Juvenile Offenders*, October 1991, p.78.

2 *International Covenant on Civil and Political Rights*, Art.6(5), December 16, 1966, 999 U.N.T.S. 171.

3 *American Convention on Human Rights*, November 22, 1969, Art.4(5), OAS Treaty Series No.36, OEA/ser.L/V/II.23, doc.21 rev.2.

4 Amnesty International, supra note 1, p.79.

5 Amnesty International, *Death Penalty News*, June 1994, p.5. Since 1985, the U.S. has executed 9 juvenile offenders: Charles Rumbaugh on 09/11/85 (TX); James Terry Roach on 01/10/86 (SC); Jay Pinkerton on 05/15/85 (TX); Dalton Prejean on 05/18/90 (LA); Johnny Frank Garrett on 02/11/92 (TX); Curtis Paul Harris on 07/01/93 (TX); Frederick Lashley on 07/27/93 (MO); Ruben Montaya Cantu on 08/24/93 (TX); and Christopher Burger on 12/07/93 (GA) (Amnesty International USA, *Death Penalty Log*, January 5, 1994, p.16).

6 408 U.S. 238 (1972).

7 Victor L. Streib, *The Juvenile Death Penalty Today*, October 20, 1994, p. 9.

8 See for example, Amnesty International, supra note 1, p.4; Paul Raeburn, "Stiff Sentence," *Omni*, February 1988, p.28; Don Colburn, "Growing Up on Death Row," *Washington Post Health*, July 19, 1988, pp.12, 14.

9 *Convention on the Rights of the Child*, Art.37(a), November 20, 1989, U.N. Doc. A/RES/44/49.

10 See for example, *International Covenant on Civil and Political Rights*, supra note 2; *American Convention on Human Rights*, supra note 3; *Convention on the Rights of the Child*, supra note 10.

11 Amnesty International, supra note 1, pp.74-75 (quoting *Twentieth Century Fund Task Force on Sentencing Policy Toward Young Offenders Confronting Youth Crime*, 1978, p.7).

[12] Ibid., p.75.

[13] See supra notes 1-3 and accompanying text; see also Amnesty International, supra note 1, p.78.

[14] *Geneva Convention Relative to the Protection of Civilian Persons in Time of War*, Art.68, August 12, 1949, 6 U.S.T. 3516, 3560, 75 U.N.T.S. 287, 330. (*Fourth Geneva Convention*)

[15] *International Covenant on Civil and Political Rights*, supra note 2.

[16] *American Convention on Human Rights* (1979), 1144 U.N.T.S. 123 O.A.S.T.S. 36.

[17] See Amnesty International, supra note 1, p.78.

[18] See David Weissbrodt, "Execution of Juvenile Offenders by the United States Violates International Human Rights Law," 3 *Am. U. J. Int'l L. & Pol'y* 339, 348 (1988).

[19] Frank Newman and David Weissbrodt, *International Human Rights: Selected International Human Rights Instruments*, 1994, Supplement, p.96.

[20] Ibid., p.96.

[21] *James Terry Roach and Jay Pinkerton*, Case 9647, para.48, Inter-Am. C.H.R. 147, 166, OEA/ser.L/V/II.71, doc.9, rev.1 (1987).

[22] *American Declaration on the Rights and Duties of Man*, May 2, 1948, Arts. I, VII, XXVI, OAS res XXX, adopted by the Ninth International Conference of American States, Bogota (1968).

[23] Case 9647, Inter-Am. C.H.R. 147, OEA/ser. L./V/II.71, doc.9, rev.1 (1987).

[24] Amnesty International, supra note 1, p.75.

[25] Ibid., p.76.

[26] Ibid., p.64.

[27] See *Thompson v. Oklahoma*, 487 U.S. 815, 830-31 and n.34 (1988); *Stanford v. Kentucky*, 492 U.S. 361, 369, and n.1 (1989).

[28] Amnesty International, supra note 1, p.64.

[29] On July 1, 1994, Kansas became the 37th U.S. state with a death penalty statute.

[30] Streib, supra note 7, p. 4.

THE REV. FRED TAYLOR

RACE, YOUTH, POVERTY AND THE DEATH PENALTY

I AM FROM the Southern Christian Leadership Conference (SCLC). My primary responsibility is that of Coordinator of Direct Action, but I also have the area of our work which deals with the abolition of the death penalty. I serve on the Board of the National Coalition to Abolish the Death Penalty.

I am appreciative of the opportunity afforded me to represent the Southern Christian Leadership Conference. Our founding president, Martin Luther King, Jr., earned his Ph.D. and matriculated at Boston University in the early 1950's. Yet, some forty years later, his *alma mater* still refuses to give his papers to his widow for the Center which she built. In my judgment, BU's posture on this issue has racist implications and manifestations.

I am here today as a part of the legacy of nonviolence for social change as espoused, preached and lived by Dr. King. An assassin took his life, and six years after his assassination, the same fate met his mother, Mrs. Albert Williams King. Yet, the King family remains uncompromisingly opposed to the death penalty, and

REVEREND FRED TAYLOR An ordained Baptist Minister, is Coordinator of the Direct Action Crisis Intervention Committee at the Southern Christian Leadership Conference. Reverend Taylor was Pastor of the Road during the Abolition of the Death Penalty Pilgrimage from Starke, Florida, to Atlanta, Georgia. He was also a Coordinator for the Re-enactment of the 1965 Selma to Montgomery March, marking the 20th Anniversary of that march, and for the Re-enactment of the 25th Anniversary of the Selma to Montgomery Movement, which led to the passage of the 1965 Voting Rights Act. Reverend Taylor is the recipient of the 1990 *Unsung Hero Award* for Outstanding Contributions to the Community, and the *Rosa Parks Award* for Outstanding Leadership in Non-violent Direct Action.

they continue to participate in the movement calling for its abolition.

I am also here today as one whose 14-year-old cousin, Derrick, shot and killed my uncle, his father, in October, 1992. My family is still in the mixture of having to cope with the dynamics of the grief caused by the killing of a loved one, and the family is divided, given Derrick's young age. Six months' probation punishment was rendered by the State of Indiana. Is that adequate justice, a segment of my family is asking.

Still, further, I am here today to reaffirm SCLC's unconditional opposition to the death penalty. Dr. Joseph Lowery, our president, is on record as saying that the death penalty has little or nothing to do with the fact of crime in this country. The administration of the death penalty has more to do, in Dr. Lowery's opinion, with race and place. In other words, if you are non-white and live in the South, and kill someone, and if your victim is white, you are most likely to get the death penalty.

Also, Dr. Lowery continues to remind the nation that capital punishment, as those of us in the abolition movement know, is for those who do not have the capital. Essentially, if you are convicted of a murder and you are poor and illiterate, you are the prime target of the death penalty.

It is most unfortunate, in my view, that the death penalty is still legal in this country, for people of any age. The 1964 Civil Rights Act was a kind of watershed in legality insofar as civil rights in the U.S. are concerned. In my view, the legal framework for social justice was expanded and strengthened with the passage of this statute and the 1965 Voting Rights Act.

I am also here as an African-American clergyman who takes the position that just as there are order, design and predictability in nature, as Dr. George Washington Carver, a scientist, understood, so, in justice, in the criminal justice system, there ought to be truth, mercy, righteousness, compassion and love.

As Dr. King reminded us, the moral arm of the universe is long, and it is bent toward justice. In our quest to become a beloved community, a complete community, a holistic community, as we seek

We at the moment are more concerned with the facts of the crime and reasons to kill our children than with the remedy—rather than attempting to remedy the reasons or conditions which lead our children to commit heinous acts.

to correct our many errors in judgment of many years, we must, as a nation, be deliberate and intentional in our commitment to care, provide and protect the children of our nation.

We at the moment are more concerned with the facts of the crime and reasons to kill our children than with the remedy—rather than attempting to remedy the reasons or conditions which lead our children to commit heinous acts. According to Dr. Victor L. Streib, Professor of Law at Cleveland State University, the deadly road of killing children in this country began back in 1642 with the execution of Thomas Graunger in Plymouth Colony, Massachusetts. In the 350 years since Brother Graunger's execution, this country has executed, state-approved, 343 persons who, at the time of their crime, were under the age of 18.[1]

Now, my brothers and sisters, in the most recent of times, nine executions of juvenile offenders have occurred since 1985, including five since 1992.[2] As you know, 1973 is the year death sentencing began under the new state statutes, following the Supreme Court's 1972 decision which struck down all then existing death penalty statutes.[3] Since 1973, 22 states have participated in this state-approved slaughter of our children.[4]

As of today (August 6, 1993), 33 juvenile offenders are still on death row. Seventeen are black, which is 52 percent. Three are Hispanic, which is 9 percent. Thirteen are white, which is 39 percent. Sixty-four percent of the victims were white. Twenty-nine percent of the victims were black, and 7 percent of the victims were Hispanic.[5] So this is a very bleak picture for our country as the world sees us.

Now, my brothers and sisters, in looking at the issues confronting the ills which cause this chilling reality in the U.S.A., let us look at some of the reasons why our people are entrapped in the criminal justice system. As of 1985, more than 50 percent of the youths in detention centers were black, compared to only 10 percent of whites as of the same year.[6]

Furthermore, the number of persons on death row in this country has more than tripled since 1980, when we had 688 people on death rows in this country.[7] Today, that number is 2,636.[8]

The U.S. criminal justice system is not color-blind. Nine-hundred-sixty-four per 100,000 African-Americans are involved in the criminal justice system, compared to 155 per 100,000 white Americans. African-Americans are present in the U.S. criminal justice system at a rate six-and-a-half times greater than white Americans.[9]

We must emphatically affirm, when talking about the economy, that it is more cost effective for the U.S. to educate its youth, house its homeless, provide medical care to its ill, feed its hungry, clothe its naked, offer hope to the despairing, offer art, culture and religion to the minds, hearts and souls of all its people, than to expend time, money and energy on the dead-end road, the senseless road, the inhumane road of the death penalty, because the death penalty has not been and is not a deterrent to crime.

Moreover, African-American youth are incarcerated at a rate five times greater than the rate of white youth.[10] In 1984 and 1988, white youth incarcerated in youth detention centers decreased by 2 percent, while the incarceration of black youth increased by 269 percent.[11] In this country, as of February 1990, 900,690 black men were in the criminal justice system, either in court or on probation, in jail or on death row, while only 436,000 were in colleges and universities, compared to just over a million young white men in the criminal justice system in this country, and over 4,600,000 young white males in our colleges and universities.[12]

So I say the moral imperative of the universe demands of me, in particular, and of all persons of conscience around the world, to ask the important question: Why does the United States allow its states to continue to kill to prove that killing is wrong?

We must emphatically affirm, when talking about the economy, that it is more cost effective for the U.S. to educate its youth, house its homeless, provide medical care to its ill, feed its hungry, clothe its naked, offer hope to the despairing, offer art, culture and religion to the minds, hearts and souls of all its people, than to expend time, money and energy on the dead-end road, the senseless road, the inhumane road of the death penalty, because the death penalty has not been and is not a deterrent to crime.

Our country continues to be out of step with the music of abolition played in most countries around the world. So, in the name of truth, justice, innocence, compassion, religion and, yes, love, I say to America, in the words of the Mosaic code, "Thou shalt not kill." That admonition is just as binding upon the United States of America not to kill its own citizens as it is upon a person who kills a police officer in a drug bust.

NOTES

1 Victor L. Streib, *The Juvenile Death Penalty Today: Present Death Row Inmates Under Juvenile Death Sentences and Death Sentences and Executions for Juvenile Crimes*, January 1, 1973, to December 31, 1993, p.2.

2 Ibid., p. 3.

3 *Furman v. Georgia*, 408 U.S. 238 (1972).

4 Streib, p.6.

5 Ibid., p.8. As of August 31, 1994, 35 juveniles were on death rows in 12 different U.S. states (Streib, *The Juvenile Death Penalty Today*, January 1, 1973, to August 31, 1994, p.9).

6 "Crime and the Nation's Response to It: Increasing Devastation and Expenditure of Public Funds With No Accompanying Benefit," NAACP Legal Defense and Educational Fund, Inc. Report, January 1993, pp. 1-2.

7 U.S. Department of Justice, Bureau of Justice Statistics, Historical Corrections Statistics in the U.S., 1850-1984. December 1986, table 2-8.

8 NAACP LDF, *Death Row, U.S.A.* (Summer 1993). As of July 20, 1994, there were 2,870 people on death rows across the U.S. (*LDF, Death Row, U.S.A.*, Summer 1994.)

9 "Crime and the Nation's Response to It," NAACP, LDF Report, p.4.

10 Ibid., p.5.

11 Ibid., The Sentencing Project.

12 Ibid.

RUTH LUCKASSON

THE DEATH PENALTY AND THOSE WITH MENTAL RETARDATION

MANY INDIVIDUALS who are sentenced to death and executed in this country have mental retardation. Mental retardation is a mental disability distinct from mental illness. Frequently there is confusion about the two disabilities in the judicial systems and among citizens of this country.

Mental retardation, in the uniformly accepted definition promulgated by the American Association on Mental Retardation, has three components: significantly subaverage intellectual functioning, accompanying impairments in the adaptive skills of the person, and manifestation of the disability before the age of 18.[1] It is, by definition, a very serious disability that affects every dimension of a person's life. People who have this disability are in the lowest one to three percent of the entire population, in terms of intelligence. These are adults in the criminal justice system who have mental ages of six, seven, eight—people with mental ages of young children.

The irony of mental retardation is that it's relatively easy to document and evaluate, unlike, for example, some types of mental ill-

RUTH LUCKASSON Professor of Special Education and Coordinator of Mental Retardation Programs at the University of New Mexico, Albuquerque; attorney. Author, co-author or editor of: *The Criminal Justice System and Mental Retardation: Defendants and Victims*; *Competence Assessment for Standing Trial for Defendants with Mental Retardation (CAST-MR)*; *Mental Retardation: Definition, Classification, and Systems of Supports* (9th Ed.). Chair of the Committee on Terminology and Classification of the American Association on Mental Retardation (AAMR).

ness. Mental retardation almost always has existed from birth or early childhood. Should investigators bother to look, they would almost always find long school histories documenting repeated testing and failure in school, and frequently medical records indicating accompanying physical disabilities. Mental retardation is not a diagnosis, were the criminal justice system interested, that would be difficult to prove.

How does mental retardation interact with the criminal justice system? Although it's difficult to generalize about every person who has mental retardation, there are some predictable behaviors and limitations that accompany such terribly impaired intelligence.

Almost uniformly, individuals with mental retardation have grave difficulties in language and communication. They have problems with attention, memory, intellectual rigidity, and in moral development or moral understanding. They are very susceptible to suggestion and readily acquiesce to other adults or authority figures. This is not surprising because a person with mental retardation is almost always the least intelligent person in the group, and logically looks to others for direction. If one is the least intelligent person in a group, a good method of adaptation is to begin at a very early age to pay attention to the signals others give or to pay attention to what authority figures say. Paying attention to what parents or older friends or older siblings say is generally an effective strategy because, when you have the least intelligence of anyone around, you have to follow someone else's lead.

People with mental retardation have limited knowledge because their impaired intelligence has prevented them from learning very much. They also have grave problems in logic, foresight, planning, strategic thinking, and understanding consequences. Beyond these disabilities is the tremendous stigma that accompanies low intelligence in our society and in almost all societies. Few are as devalued or as stigmatized as the least intelligent person in a group. In our society, for example, the most common insults directed at people with mental retardation have to do with low intelligence. Thus devalued by others, people with mental retardation tend to internalize that devaluation.[2]

Considering what mental retardation is, the limitations accompanying it, and the nature of the imposition of the death penalty in the United States, can you imagine anyone easier to execute than the person I have just described? Are there any other characteristics more applicable to basic questions of blameworthiness or culpability than those characteristics?

How many people with mental retardation are accused of capital crimes in the United States? The horror is we don't know. We do know the number of people with mental retardation in the criminal justice system is roughly equal to the number of people with mental retardation in the general population, something like one to three percent.[3] However, we don't know how many of those have been accused of capital crimes or executed.

Defendants with mental retardation do not get thorough evaluations. Most people with mental retardation don't have physical markers indicating their mental retardation, thus their mental limitations are ignored, interpreted away, or used to unjustly convict them. Good investigations are not conducted in these cases, so even what should be the routine collection of an individual's school and medical records is not done. The families of people with mental retardation are not interviewed and family medical histories are not taken.

Forensic psychiatrists and forensic psychologists, for the most part, evaluate for mental illness (to the extent they evaluate for anything). So while they may conclude a person does not have mental illness, that is rarely the issue for a person who has mental retardation. Defendants with mental retardation are missed routinely by the forensic evaluators who ought to recognize them.

Police officers, judges, prosecutors and even the clients' own defense lawyers fail to pick up on the mental retardation. This

Consider each step of a capital proceeding, and superimpose on each step significantly impaired intelligence. You will have some idea of why a person with mental retardation, once caught in the system, cannot escape.

occurs in part because the individuals themselves often attempt to hide their stigmatizing disabilities, and because they innocently cooperate with the very system that is trying to kill them.

Testimony of death-row survivors shows it took years of work and intelligence, resources and strength to escape the grips of the system. It would be a feat impossible to accomplish if they had mental retardation.

Consider each step of a capital proceeding, and superimpose on each step significantly impaired intelligence. You will have some idea of why a person with mental retardation, once caught in the system, cannot escape.

Reliable questioning after a crime is often prevented by the confusion, lack of understanding, communication and memory impairments of a person with mental retardation. At the arrest stage, individuals with mental retardation frequently exhibit extreme gullibility. They often look for direction from the police officer, whom they see as a friend and authority figure, without thinking about how to protect themselves from that officer.

Confessions and statements given by a person with mental retardation raise the same issues. Techniques that might not be coercive to a person without mental retardation will often coerce a person who is so impaired. For example, a man in Texas who had mental retardation and was executed last year, described to me, in very accepting terms, how he happened to give a damaging statement to the police. He said when he was in custody, the police officers put their guns on the table, told him to "go for it," and said to him, "I tell you what, Nigger, I'll gun you down on the spot." It was then he gave his statement. Other people might have been able to resist that kind of pressure from a police officer, but this defendant, with his very low IQ and his mental retardation, was not.

Hiring a lawyer costs money. People with mental retardation have almost no ability to hire lawyers, or direct or monitor the kind of legal representation they receive.

Investigation that includes an examination of medical, educational, and social records in the case of people with mental retardation is absolutely essential. A skilled investigator is crucial be-

I have seen people with mental retardation sitting in their own capital trials, with their lives at stake, who had absolutely no understanding of what was going on.

cause individuals with mental retardation are typically unable to supply the details and chronology of their lives.

Even in something as simple as plea bargaining, a person who, because of impaired intelligence, does not know the difference between more and less, is in no position to accept or reject a plea bargain. At the trial itself, this person is greatly disadvantaged. I have seen people with mental retardation sitting in their own capital trials, with their lives at stake, who had absolutely no understanding of what was going on.

I remember very clearly the case of a mother watching her son with mental retardation standing trial for his life. One could see she had given a lot of thought to what she could do to comfort him, or to make some connection with this son who had such a low I.Q. Finally, the one thing she found to do all day was to give him a small candy bar. That, at least, was something he could understand during his trial.

At another capital trial, a man with mental retardation stood on his feet in sheer terror throughout the entire proceeding. He feared every move, whether from a room to his jail cell, or to a car, or to some space in the courtroom. He had some superficial understanding of the electric chair and believed he could be electrocuted wherever he sat, whether in a car, at his lawyer's table, or anywhere, and that any person around him could flip a switch and electrocute him. That terror, directly related to his mental retardation, consumed him during his trial.

NOTES

1 Luckasson, R., Coulter, D.L., Polloway, E.A., Reiss, S., Schalock, R.L., Snell, M.E., Spitalnik, D.M., & Stark, J.A. (1992). *Mental Retardation: Definition, Classification, and Systems of Supports*. Washington, D.C.: American Association on Mental Retardation.

2 *See generally*, Ellis, J.W., & Luckasson, R. (1985), "Mentally Retarded Criminal Defendants," *The George Washington Law Review*, 53, 414-493.

3 Noble, J.H. Jr., & Conley, R.W. (1992), "Toward an Epidemiology of Relevant Attributes," in R.W. Conley, R. Luckasson, & G.N. Bouthilet (Eds.), *The Criminal Justice System and Mental Retardation: Defendants and Victims*. Baltimore: Paul H. Brookes Publishing.

HUGO ADAM BEDAU

INNOCENCE AND THE DEATH PENALTY

WESTERN CIVILIZATION, one might say, begins and is founded on two great pillars of execution of the innocent, the execution of the philosopher Socrates by the Athenians in the year 399 BC on charges for which he was not guilty, and the execution of Jesus of Nazareth in the early years of this era for crimes under the Romans for which he was not guilty.

In more recent years the execution of the innocent has played a significant role in the quarrel over the death penalty. Two-hundred-and-fifty years ago in France great alarm and great controversy arose over the execution of Jean Calas, whose innocence was established after his death.[1] Not many years ago Great Britain's government acknowledged that the execution of Timothy Evans was erroneous, because another man had in fact committed those crimes.[2]

What is the story on this theme in the United States? No other aspect of the death penalty, it would appear, has aroused the interest of the American public as this issue has. Survey research of American public attitudes shows that of all the various questions

HUGO ADAM BEDAU Austin B. Fletcher Professor of Philosophy, Tufts University; Vice Chairman of the Board, National Coalition to Abolish the Death Penalty (NCADP). Author, co-author or editor of: *In Spite of Innocence*, 1992; *The Death Penalty in America*, 1964, revised ed. 1967, 3rd edition, 1982; *Capital Punishment in the United States*, 1976; *The Courts, The Constitution, and Capital Punishment*, 1977; *Death is Different: Studies in the Morality, Law and Politics of Capital Punishment*, 1987. Delegate to Stockholm International Conference on the Death Penalty, sponsored by Amnesty International, December 1977. Expert witness before: legislative committees on bills to repeal or reintroduce the death penalty in several U.S. states, and both the U.S. House of Representatives and the Senate.

addressed—the issue of racial bias, the issue of deterrence, the issue of cost—none so interests those who haven't quite made up their mind, or who aren't quite thoroughly convinced of the need for vengeance, as the possibility of executing the innocent, and well it might.

All decent people oppose the execution of the innocent. That is why the United States Government, Department of Justice, took out after me and my colleague, Professor Michael Radelet, when, six years ago, we published research in a law review recounting the deplorable record of conviction of the innocent, sentencing to death of the innocent, and indeed executing the innocent in this country in this century.[3]

The only research that the United States Government has ever criticized involving the quarrel over the death penalty is this research. I believe the reason for its criticism is that it is recognized that this is of major continuing concern to the public.

Three aspects of this problem exist, as seen from the direction of those who disagree with me. These kinds of criticism are not often heard, but they are heard here and there in the country by those who defend the death penalty when confronted with this issue.

Throughout this century, in every jurisdiction except for six or seven of the smallest states in the United States, innocent people have been convicted of capital crimes, and innocent people have been sentenced to death for them. There is nothing to discuss.

The first thing they say is: Even if it is possible that an innocent person could be executed, there is no proof that any have been. In reply I would say it is correct that no branch of the government, executive, legislative or judiciary, state or federal in the United States, has admitted that anyone has been executed who was innocent.

There is no record in this century of any branch of the government, state or federal, admitting to the execution of the innocent in the 20th century. There is a record, however, of the admission of the execution of the innocent in the 19th century, but let's treat that as ancient history.

What we can infer from this silence, of course, is very little. Governments have admitted, both at the legislative, executive and judicial levels, in state and federal jurisdictions, especially the state jurisdictions, that many, many people have been innocent but convicted of capital crimes, innocent but convicted and sentenced to death for capital crimes.

On that point critics have no case. The record is abundantly clear. Throughout this century, in every jurisdiction except for six or seven of the smallest states in the United States, innocent people have been convicted of capital crimes, and innocent people have been sentenced to death for them. There is nothing to discuss.

In particular, many of these cases, approximately two dozen, involve rescue from the execution chamber with less than three days to spare.[4] In several cases, as recently as the past decade, there have been people within hours of execution under law who were not executed, and it was later established that they were innocent.[5]

Are we to believe that the demonstrated incontestible record of persons who were innocent but convicted and sentenced to death and carried right to the door of the execution chamber, never crossed the threshold and anyone innocent executed? Are we seriously to believe this?

What, after all, counts as proof of the execution of the innocent? That the person who supposedly was the murder victim walks in off the street? That has happened, but not in the 20th century in the United States. That is a very, very rare occurrence. It has not happened in any of the 23 cases that Michael Radelet and I have reported where we believe an innocent person was executed.

Where, finally, is the forum in which this issue is to be thrashed out? No judicial forum exists under American law, state or federal, for the determination of the innocence of somebody who is in his grave. No such forum is about to be created.

We will have this issue before us in the posture of a disputed question of history forever. Historians will quarrel over whether in fact the people whom we think are innocent but executed really were innocent, and there is no resolution of that dispute in sight. Meanwhile, the record of persons innocent and convicted, innocent, convicted and sentenced to death, marches on.

The second argument of those who defend the death penalty by criticizing the possibility of executing the innocent, is: Even if the innocent have been executed, for the sake of the argument, there is virtually no risk of that today; it can't happen now.

Now, it is true that of the 23 cases that my colleague and I cite in our research which has now been made available in this book, *In Spite of Innocence*,[6] (which is much more readable than the law review article in which it was originally published), many are by and large older cases.

Why is it that the defenders of the death penalty say that the risk has become so low? Their explanation is that procedural reforms developed over the past 20 years under the leadership of the United States Supreme Court make it virtually impossible for anyone to be convicted who is innocent, sentenced to death who is innocent, and above all executed who is innocent.

They are laws that not only result in the continuing discrimination and arbitrariness of the death penalty, but also result in the continuing conviction of the innocent, and nothing in the future that is a possible area of reform of the criminal law in the United States is going to change this matter.

I submit that this is nonsense, not merely wrong, but nonsense. The record of the Supreme Court's deliberations on the death penalty over the last 20 years, beginning with *Furman v. Georgia*,[7] have resulted in a series of procedural reforms and appellate practices designed primarily to address one issue, the arbitrariness of the death penalty, the arbitrariness with which it is carried out by the courts. The risk of executing the innocent is supposed to take care of itself.

The laws governing conviction, the laws governing decision of sentence, the laws governing all aspects of the trial have not been altered by the United States Supreme Court. They are laws that not only result in the continuing discrimination and arbitrariness of the death penalty, but also result in the continuing conviction of the innocent, and nothing in the future that is a possible area of reform of the criminal law in the United States is going to change this matter.

There are not going to be decisions by the bar or the courts or the legislatures to bar circumstantial evidence. There are not going to be decisions to rule out confessions of the guilty, but this is exactly how the innocent get convicted. They falsely confess. Suborned testimony is used against them. Exculpating evidence is withheld from their attorneys. Incompetent attorneys are appointed.

This is the dreadful litany of the causation of the errors of justice that sentence innocent people to death. Nothing the United States Supreme Court has done has touched any of these causes. Nothing it will do will touch these causes. So the problem of the risk of error is chronic and unremediable.

The third thing defenders of the death penalty frequently say is: Even if there is a risk, it is worth it. Why is the risk of the death penalty worth it? Is it because we get incarceration and incapacitation that we cannot get any other way? Is it because we get deterrence that we cannot get by any other method? Is it because it is cheaper? Is it because it is fairer? Is it because the public deserves it? Not a single one of those questions can be seriously answered in the affirmative. It is simply false that the risk is worth it.

NOTES

[1] See generally D. Bien, *The Calas Affair: Persecution, Toleration, and Heresy in Eighteenth Century Toulouse* (1960); E. Nixon, *Voltaire and the Calas Case* (1961).

[2] See generally L. Kennedy, *Ten Rillington Place* (1961).

[3] Hugo Adam Bedau and Michael L. Radelet, "Miscarriages of Justice in Potentially Capital Cases," *Stanford Law Review*, Vol.40, No.1 (November 1987), pp.21-179.

[4] Ibid., p.72.

[5] See for example, Joseph Green Brown, who came within 13 hours of execution before being released on the grounds of innocence in 1987 (Michael L. Radelet, Hugo Adam Bedau, and Constance E. Putnam, *In Spite of Innocence: Erroneous Convictions in Capital Cases*, Ithaca, Northeastern University Press, 1992, pp.290-91).

[6] Ibid.

[7] 408 U.S. 238 (1972).

RONALD HAMPTON

THE DEATH PENALTY: RACIAL BIAS, COST, AND THE RISK OF EXECUTING THE INNOCENT

I AM the executive director of the National Black Police Association (NBPA), which is an advocacy organization for African-American police officers and the African-American community. The NBPA addresses issues and concerns that have a negative impact on the African-American community. It was established to improve the relationship between police departments as institutions and the African-American community, and to act as a mechanism to recruit African-Americans and other minority police officers on a national scale as well as to work toward police reform in order to eliminate police corruption, brutality and racial discrimination. One of the most important concerns of the NBPA is the issue of the death penalty in America.

The National Black Police Association believes that the death penalty is un-American, unjust and unconstitutional. Currently, over 2,800 U.S. citizens are on death row (the highest number in U.S. history).[1] Nearly all of these people are poor.

RONALD E. HAMPTON Executive Director, National Black Police Association; 20-year veteran of the Washington, D.C. Metropolitan Police Department. Specialist in developing and teaching skills to national and international communities in the areas of community relations, crime prevention, and human rights. Served as Consultant in community relations/crime prevention for the U.S. Department of Justice, Community Relations Service. Lecturer, American University's Washington Semester School, Criminal Justice Program. Board Member: Amnesty International USA; Drug Policy Foundation's Law Enforcement Committee; National Advisory Board for Humanitas; ACLU Advisory Committee, Capital Punishment Project; Citizens United for the Rehabilitation of Errants (CURE), Texas State Chapter Advisory Board; NCADP.

...the death penalty is almost exclusively reserved as a tool for white retribution. This sends a clear message that when people of color—particularly black people—are killed, whether as victims of private or state-sanctioned homicide, the cost to society is hardly as great as when whites are killed.

The Bureau of Justice and the National Association for the Advancement of Colored People (NAACP) statistics show that between 1930 and 1990, 4,016 people were executed in the United States.[2] Of this number, 2,129 (53%) were black.[3] Black men were also much more likely to be executed for rape than any other group. Of 455 men executed for rape between 1930 and 1976, 405 (90%) were black.[4] On average during this time, only 12% of the nation's population was black. Today, while the percentage of African-Americans in the general population remains at about 12%, approximately 40% of the people on death row are black.[5]

Since 1972, 85% of those executed were convicted of killing white victims; whereas during the same time span, nearly half of all homicide victims were black.[6] In fact, since capital punishment was re-instituted in 1976, only one white defendant has been executed for killing a non-white victim.[7] In other words, the death penalty is almost exclusively reserved as a tool for white retribution. This sends a clear message that when people of color—particularly black people—are killed, whether as victims of private or state-sanctioned homicide, the cost to society is hardly as great as when whites are killed.

One may respond by saying the solution to this endemic racial bias in the application of the death penalty is to attempt to ensure that more people who are convicted of murdering people of color receive the death penalty. However, this is no easier to accomplish than it is to cure racial bias in the overall criminal justice system as a whole.

In 1987, researchers documented 350 cases in the 20th century where 325 defendants whose guilt was in serous doubt were convicted of murder and 119 of these very likely innocent people were sentenced to death.[8] The same study found the state of New York to lead in erroneous convictions. Kirk Bloodsworth celebrated his independence as a free man recently. After serving nine years and being sentenced to death, a DNA test established that he was innocent of the crime. His vindication is to be applauded, but the fact that others like him may still be on death row remains the strongest argument against capital punishment. Also, there is the story of Walter McMillian, freed in March 1993 after serving five years, under a death sentence in an Alabama prison, for a crime he did not commit.

There is no doubt that innocent people are sometimes convicted on the testimony of both well-meaning and not so well-meaning individuals. People serving sentences can be freed and compensated when the truth is uncovered, but there can be no justice or compensation for those whose death sentences already have been carried out by the state.

Proponents of the death penalty suggest that capital punishment means fewer murders, especially of police officers. FBI statistics for the period 1976-1985 prove just the opposite.[9] In the 12 states where executions took place, the murder rate was 106 per million, exactly twice the murder rate—53 per million—of the 13 states without the death penalty. More police officers per capita were killed in states with the death penalty than in states without the death penalty.

The death penalty escapes the decisive cost-benefit analysis to which every other program is held. Rather than being posed as a single, but costly, alternative in a spectrum of approaches to crime, the death penalty operates at the extremes of political rhetoric.

The exorbitant costs of capital punishment are actually making America less safe because badly needed financial and legal resources are being diverted from proven, effective crime-fighting strategies such as community policing. While recession cuts into the core of this nation's crime fighting arsenal, hundreds of millions of dollars are being spent on capital punishment with no reduction in violent crime. At the source, police forces are being cut, prisoners released early because of overcrowding and delayed trials in an underfunded justice system.

The death penalty escapes the decisive cost-benefit analysis to which every other program is held. Rather than being posed as a single, but costly, alternative in a spectrum of approaches to crime, the death penalty operates at the extremes of political rhetoric. Having a death penalty is much more expensive than life imprisonment without parole.[10] Capital punishment is costly largely because almost everyone facing the penalty will go to trial, whereas in other criminal cases, about 90% enter guilty pleas instead.

The driving force behind the death penalty in this country are politicians who use the issue in an attempt to appear tough on crime. Our criminal justice system is breaking down for lack of direction and funds while some pour more money into the black hole of capital punishment. The death penalty does not prevent crime. The fear of apprehension and the prospect of swift and certain punishment provide the largest deterrent to crime.

As a twenty-year veteran of the Washington, D.C. Metropolitan Police Department, I have witnessed first-hand every conceivable act of violence. I have buried fellow police officers and friends killed in the line of duty. I have consoled grieving mothers whose babies have been brutally beaten on their doorstep. I have comforted youths witnessing their mothers and fathers taken to jail. Despite all that, I have yet to witness any crime that in my opinion warrants the death penalty. Violence only begets violence.

NOTES

[1] NAACP Legal Defense and Educational Fund, Inc., *Death Row, U.S.A.* (Spring 1994).
[2] U.S. Department of Justice, *Correctional Populations in the U.S., 1991*, p.134.
[3] Ibid.
[4] LDF/ACLU videotape, *Double Justice*, 1993.
[5] LDF, *Death Row, U.S.A.* (Spring 1994).
[6] NAACP Legal Defense and Educational Fund, Inc., *Execution Update*, June 23, 1994.
[7] Ibid.
[8] Hugo Adam Bedau and Michael L. Radelet, "Miscarriages of Justice in Potentially Capital Cases," *Stanford Law Review* Vol. 40, No.1 (Nov. 1987), p.38.
[9] *FBI Uniform Crime Reports* (Washington D.C.: U.S. Department of Justice, 1986), p.10.
[10] Richard C. Dieter, *Millions Misspent: What Politicians Don't Say About the High Costs of the Death Penalty* (Washington, D.C.: Death Penalty Information Center, 1992).

MARLENE KAMISH

THE CASE OF MANUEL SALAZAR

MANUEL SALAZAR was unjustly charged in the death of a policeman. He acted in self-defense after a brutal beating and after the policeman attempted to kill him. Several months ago, Ron Hampton, Executive Director of the National Black Police Association, came to see Manuel Salazar where he sits on death row in Pontiac, Illinois. The guards at the gates were considerably surprised to see Ron Hampton there to visit Manuel Salazar. It was not their usual experience. And it was a great reassurance to Manuel to have support from Ron Hampton and his organization, particularly in the context of Manuel's case.

Manuel Salazar is a 27-year-old innocent Latino under sentence of death. Manuel is in Pontiac in the condemned unit as a result of racist action by law enforcement in Joliet and as a result of a racist prosecution in the State of Illinois.

I spoke with Manuel on a conference line from my office only a few minutes ago. He sends his love and gratitude to this tribunal. He has great courage, and he rarely lets me witness any wavering of confidence. He assures me that he does not suffer, and I am speechless. He says that he has food, though he admits that he is sometimes hungry. He tells me that he has a home, though he has only a cell with three concrete walls, one wall of bars, and a two-step walk from the wall to his bed. He tells me that he is loved and he

MARLENE KAMISH Attorney for Illinois death-row inmate, Manuel Salazar, is President of and attorney for For The Defense, a Chicago-based, non-profit legal office acting in cases of manifest injustice.

has great faith. So he says it is a sin to call it suffering. He tells me that because he is an artist and can paint and express himself to his people through his art, he is free.

This is the man the State of Illinois intends to execute. When I say his case is pervaded by racism, I know whereof I speak. Manuel was riding in a car with his friends at five o'clock in the afternoon of September 12, 1984. The police report of the incident says that the car was noticed by the police and stopped for one reason: "Negroes and Spanish were seen in the car together." For that reason the car was considered to be suspicious.

Manuel ran from the car because he had a gun in his gym bag. He had been target practicing down by the river. The policeman chased him with his gun drawn. The policeman never knew Manuel had a gun. It was in the bag he was carrying, and it was found over the fence. The policeman trapped Manuel by the fence. The policeman did what Joliet policemen frequently do, which is the reason I think that this case has become so important in Joliet. The policeman hit Manuel in the eye and dropped him by the fence. He fell on top of him, beat him mercilessly, placing his knee in his stomach. Manuel succeeded in pushing the policeman off him. Then the policeman pulled his gun and said he was going to kill Manuel. They struggled over the gun, and in that struggle the policeman died. The autopsy report of the policeman shows that the policeman had been drinking—an unsavory fact for the police department in Joliet to have to deal with.

There was a knife strapped to the policeman's leg. We can presume from that fact that the policeman intended for Manuel to die. Since Manuel was unarmed, the policeman would have to leave that knife on Manuel to justify his own actions.

Manuel described the pain he suffered and the fear and dazed condition he felt after the incident. He described running from the scene and jumping into a creek and going to a friend's house. One friend said Manuel was unrecognizable; he looked like he had been run over by a truck. Another described him as looking like Frankenstein.

There was a shoot-to-kill order put out on the street for Manuel. Manuel was taken by people who love him to Mexico, where he stayed with family until he was kidnapped on May 18, 1985. Early on that May morning, armed men surrounded the house in Mexico. They grabbed Manuel from his bed. They threw him out onto the street and into a car. He told me he was crying, telling people, "Look, they will kill me if they take me back." Before nightfall he was across the border in Laredo. He was taken back to Illinois, returned to the United States in violation of the treaty between the United States and Mexico. There were no legal proceedings.

An attorney who had worked for the police solicited the case from Manuel's family. The family, not knowing of this attorney's connection to the police, paid him $20,000 to save their son.

During Manuel's testimony the prosecution mocked his Mexican origin, stereotyped him, denied even the fact that the young man was religious. The prosecutor had the arrogance and duplicity to suggest that Manuel had no faith.

A most compelling indictment of our judicial system occurred in the post-conviction process where enormous evidence of Manuel's innocence was put before the Court.

The case was changed in venue from Joliet, Illinois—where there was a large Mexican community very much aware of police harassment and the kind of treatment Manuel had to endure—to Bloomington, Illinois, where an all-white jury tried and sentenced him to death. The jury found Manuel's life to be of no value, or of insufficient value to preclude the penalty of death, according to the law. The Illinois Supreme Court, with two dissenters, affirmed the conviction. Justice Clark, speaking for the dissent, stated that the rules of evidence had been bent because the victim was a policeman. The case was denied hearing by the United States Supreme Court.

A most compelling indictment of our judicial system occurred in the post-conviction process where enormous evidence of Manuel's innocence was put before the Court. Witnesses did come forward then, family came forward and teachers came forward, but our racist court still could not see, in spite of that evidence, what was patently obvious to anyone who wasn't racist, that Manuel was both innocent and truly to be valued.

Manuel's death sentence was affirmed. We are now on appeal to the Illinois Supreme Court.[1]

Amnesty International in London has written to the Governor of Illinois asking for an investigation of the process by which the treaty between the United States and Mexico was circumvented. A letter has gone from Amnesty International in London to the State Department. Others have also gone to the President of Mexico and the Foreign Minister of Mexico, the Department of Human Rights, and the Governor of Nuevo Leon, the place from which Manuel was kidnapped.

NOTES

[1] On September 22, 1994, in a six to one decision, the Illinois Supreme Court reversed Manuel Salazar's case and remanded it for a new trial.

THOMAS JOHNSON

WHEN PROSECUTORS SEEK THE DEATH PENALTY

FOR 12 YEARS, from 1979 to 1991, I was the elected prosecutor in Minneapolis, Minnesota. I would like to share with you my perceptions and observations on how a prosecutor's office makes decisions in major cases, including death penalty cases.

You should realize that Minnesota is one of 14 states in the U.S. that does not presently have a death penalty.[1] So, but for the operation of the federal death penalty within our state, neither prosecutor, judge, nor jury would be faced with having to make a capital punishment decision in the State of Minnesota. I believe I have some insight into how a large prosecutor's office operates and, from my personal experience, now as a private lawyer in the *pro bono* representation of death penalty cases, can place that insight in the perspective of capital punishment cases.

In almost all jurisdictions and all states throughout the United States, prosecutors are elected. There are very few jurisdictions in which that is not true (New Jersey, Alaska, and maybe another state or two). But for the most part, the prosecutor is an elected official, and it is that prosecutor's decision which triggers the seeking of the death penalty. The balance of the process that exists—and continues for ten years on average—exists as a check on the

THOMAS L. JOHNSON Lawyer in private practice in Minneapolis, Minnesota. Board Member: American Prosecutors Research Institute, Prosecuting Attorneys Research Council, Minnesota Advocates for Human Rights, Minnesota State Bar Association. Recipient of 1989 Minnesota Advocates for Human Rights Award. Author of numerous journal and newspaper articles on criminal justice and other public policy issues.

Significant media attention given to the murder of a young child of an affluent white family will trigger a very different reaction from a prosecutor from a case that gets little media attention and involves a victim from a poorer community.

prosecutor's initial decision. Unless a prosecutor decides that he or she will seek the death penalty, no death penalty case or prosecution will follow. Therefore, within our system, that initial decision which is invariably made by the prosecutor (even though the actual case might be handled by an assistant) is extremely critical.

The decision to seek the death penalty will be a political one, or will have a political context to it. The context may be dictated by promises the prosecutor made during an election campaign or by cases which preceded the present one within the office. For example, there might have been a significant case recently lost for which the prosecutor seeks to regain public confidence.

The way in which the case is portrayed in the media will have a critical impact on whether the prosecutor seeks a death penalty. Significant media attention given to the murder of a young child of an affluent white family will trigger a very different reaction from a prosecutor from a case that gets little media attention and involves a victim from a poorer community.

The decision made within this political context and with these kinds of factors coming into play, is unilateral. No collegial decision-making process exists here. In all instances it is the elected prosecutor who makes the decision. And it will be a decision, particularly if it is a high profile case, that will be very difficult to reverse. The prosecutor's first statement to the press, when very little is actually known about the facts of the case, might well dictate how the case is handled. Prosecutors don't like to come charging out of the starting block only to pull up short later and say, "We're throwing in the towel. We'll take a life sentence, or we'll take a plea to a lesser count than a capital homicide."

In a low profile case more latitude exists. It becomes possible to discuss a plea bargain, or to cut a deal for a guilty plea in exchange for a sentence more lenient than capital punishment. Almost invariably these deals are struck around the factually stronger, not the weaker, cases. Factually weaker cases are the ones most likely to go to trial. So, in most instances, the persons who consider themselves most culpable are willing to enter a plea. They are the ones who escape the death penalty.

The decision to seek a death sentence will also depend on time and place. Prosecutors' offices have very little institutional memory. As a newly elected prosecutor comes into office, she or he often brings new policies and new priorities along. The decision may very well depend on whether a particular homicide occurred before or after the new prosecutor was sworn in, and on whether that new prosecutor strongly favors or disfavors the death penalty. It certainly will depend on the location of the crime, as much within a state as within the different regions of our country. The State of Minnesota has 87 counties. I can tell you there would be 87 different views on when prosecutors should seek a death sentence, if we had capital punishment in the State of Minnesota.

I represented the largest jurisdiction within Minnesota. It is probably safe to say that a homicide in that jurisdiction would not look as egregious or be as sensational as a homicide in a county where homicides occur only once every decade. And a prosecutor in such a county might feel compelled, politically, to seek the death penalty.

The decision to seek the death penalty is dependent in the first instance on the time and place, and in the second instance on the political context in which a prosecutor makes his or her decision. By my way of thinking, that is the definition of "arbitrary": some-

---

Without the operation of the death penalty, I believe many prosecutors would play roles as moral agents of change within their communities. They would be advocates for a system of justice that truly seeks justice and for a system that has the strength to exercise compassion.

---

thing dependent upon where it happens, when it happens, and with a political, very subjective context in which it happened.

The problem is with the decision made, not with the prosecutor making it. Mine is a case against the way in which our system currently operates, not a suggestion that the system should be improved upon.

The death penalty is very destructive of prosecutors' offices. Without the operation of the death penalty, I believe many prosecutors would play roles as moral agents of change within their communities. They would be advocates for a system of justice that truly seeks justice and for a system that has the strength to exercise compassion.

However, the opportunity to play a role as an agent of change is destroyed when our laws and, sadly, our society dictate that a person seeking election to a position as prosecutor must stoop during the campaign not only to justifying and promoting support for the death penalty, but also to talking about how aggressively he or she would use it. This effectively undermines the kind of rational, productive discussion that needs to occur if we are to confront the true causes of violence in our society today.

So, while prosecutors are very willing to use the death penalty as a tool, I think it is also a tool that uses them, and does so destructively.

NOTES

[1] As of July 1, 1994, when Kansas became the 37th U.S. state with a death penalty statute, there are 13 states and the District of Columbia in the U.S. without a death penalty.

THE REV. JOSEPH INGLE

STATE-SANCTIONED KILLING IS A MATTER OF RACE

I HAVE STRUGGLED as someone who for nineteen years has worked with men and women on death row in the United States, who has had twenty of my good friends through this ministry exterminated by the state, and who has recorded thirteen of those stories in a book.

So I want to say that the most difficult thing for white people in this country to talk about when we talk about state-sanctioned killing is the matter of race. This is all about race. No matter what anyone may say about vengeance or deterrence, it is a matter of social control. That is what we're talking about here, and let's be clear about this.

I do not want to burden you with a lot of facts. I just want to give you one fact which tells all you need to know about the death penalty in the United States. This fact comes from the research of Watt Espy, who has devoted a major portion of his life to documenting the history of executions in the United States. In talking about the history of executions in the United States, Mr. Espy says, "Perhaps this degree of slaughter has not captured the attention of the American public because the country has been numbed by the 18,766 executions in this nation since the first one in 1608." Racism has accompanied this shameful march for nearly 400 years, and it is clearly revealed in one statistic: Only 30 white people out

REVEREND JOSEPH B. INGLE A United Church of Christ minister, and director of the Tennessee Coalition to Abolish State Killings, has worked with death-row prisoners in the American South for the last 20 years.

...the most difficult thing for white people in this country to talk about when we talk about state-sanctioned killing is the matter of race. This is all about race. No matter what anyone may say about vengeance or deterrence, it is a matter of social control. That is what we're talking about here, and let's be clear about this.

of the 18,766 people executed in the United States between 1739 and 1944 were executed for killing African-Americans. That's 30 white people out of all those executions. And of those 30 white people convicted and executed, ten murdered slaves and two of those ten were slave owners, prosecuted for destroying their property under the laws of the day, not for the destruction of black life.[1] This fact is the heart of the matter.

I was with John Spenkelink's mother at the time of his execution and had to inform her that her son had been exterminated by the State of Florida. One of the things John had said to me before his death, which echoes right up to today is, "Joe, they're going to get me first. I'm white, but there are a lot of black faces back there on death row, and that's what this is really about."

He was right. The real truth is, it's not just the faces on death row, but the fact that the people who are threatened in this country who are white, the majority, use the death penalty as a means of social control over the people they feel are threatening them.

This is not an original concept of mine. I refer you to a man who came to this country in 1828, a man named Alexis de Tocqueville, a Frenchman who spent nine months here, wrote a classic work on American democracy called *Democracy in America*. Chapter 15 of the first volume of *Democracy in America*, Tocqueville entitles, "The Tyranny of the Majority." As Tocqueville pointed out so long ago, we have the tyranny of the white majority in existence in this country. It is a tyranny based on the simple fact of race. Tocqueville pointed to the treatment of American Indians and Africans in this country, who were slaves, and he pointed out that whatever the white majority wanted to do with these folks, they could do because the white majority wrote the laws, the white majority exerted power as to who were the judges. They controlled all three branches of government. They defined the social reality of the country. Tocqueville said he feared for the future of this country because of the reality of the tyranny of the majority. What we see with the death penalty is white tyranny of the majority over the racial minorities in this country.

It's no accident that we are talking about the death penalty today in terms of race. From 1444, for approximately 400 years, European ships engaged in slavery, removing Africans from Africa. For the last 250 of those years, beginning in 1619, Africans were brought to this country, first to Virginia, then throughout the early colonies, and they were enslaved. From this period in the American experience to the end of the Civil War, three-and-a-half million black people were brought to this country. At the end of the American Civil War, three-and-a-half million black people were in this country; a half million were "free." Three million were slaves or recently freed at the end of that war.

Over that 400-year period, forty million Africans were seized from Africa by white, colonial, European and American trading ships and sent into slavery, not only to the United States but throughout the Caribbean and South America.[2] Forty million people were snatched from their homes, taken to pens, put on slave ships and taken from their country. That is what lies at the heart of this.

I grew up in the State of North Carolina, and I now live in Tennessee—and I am grateful that we had a civil rights movement. But if anyone thinks there is civil rights justice in this country when it comes to the criminal justice system, they need to think again, because it ain't there. There ain't no justice in the justice system.

In *McCleskey v. Kemp*, Supreme Court Justice Lewis Powell said, "This evidence of racism is overwhelming, it's not refuted, but what are we supposed to do, declare the whole system unconstitutional?"[3] The answer to Justice Powell was, "Of course, yes, that's what you should do." But, Justice Powell, being a white man from Richmond, Virginia, stepped away from that decision and cast the deciding vote against Warren McCleskey, not because of a lack of evidence but because of his own biases toward black people.

That is what is at the heart of this engine that we're talking about today, what Tocqueville described so accurately as the tyranny of the majority. Culpability. We are culpable as white people, so we are not going to talk about it. We are not going to have this honest discussion we're having now in a public forum.

The public forums we have in this country through the media and the press do not want this word out. They do not want it discussed. No one wants to talk about this because what can you say to people you brought to this country and enslaved? What can you tell them when, at the end of a war that freed them, you wouldn't even give them forty acres and a mule, you just set them free, and they ended up in sharecropping? What are you going to say to the American Indian whose land you stole? How can you answer those questions?

You cannot answer them unless you're willing to lay yourself open and have an honest discussion. You'd much rather indulge in a system that maintains the status quo, even if it involves systematic extermination of human beings, which the death penalty does. That's what we're talking about. In order to understand the magnitude of this, you have to think of it in terms of what we have done with the slave trade, how we came to where we are, and what I referred to briefly in my historical sketch.

In order to understand the psychological ramifications of what we're doing in this country today, you have to look to the Third Reich. Anyone who reads the Supreme Court decision in *Herrera v. Collins* (U.S. Supreme Court, decided January 25, 1993), cannot help but be reminded of Nazi Germany. In the *Herrera* decision, the highest court in the land of the United States said essentially that late evidence of innocence is irrelevant.

That is what we are facing here. The laws have been molded and warped to assist in the systematic extermination of human beings, and it's happening at a faster pace year after year after year.

Some of you may have heard of Mr. John Demjanjuk. The Israeli Supreme Court unanimously ruled that he was not Ivan the Terrible. Do you know what would have happened if his case had come before our United States Supreme Court? According to their own rules in *Herrera*, Mr. Demjanjuk would never have had an evidentiary hearing, and he would have been executed, despite the evidence that he was not Ivan the Terrible. The man was not even entitled to an evidentiary hearing under the laws of the United States Government. That is what we are facing here. The laws have been molded and warped to assist in the systematic extermination of human beings, and it's happening at a faster pace year after year after year.

We, in the abolitionist movement, cannot adequately get the word out about the death penalty in the United States. Not from lack of hard work, not from lack of truth, not from lack of trying. We simply don't have the levers of power, and we're not going to get them any time soon.

NOTES

[1] Michael L. Radelet, "Executions of Whites For Crimes Against Blacks: Exceptions to the Rule?", *The Sociological Quarterly*, Vol. 30, No. 4, 1989, p.534.
Ed. note: Since this research was conducted, one white man has been executed for killing an African-American. Donald Gaskins was put to death by the state of South Carolina in 1991. (*New York Times*, September 7, 1991, p.1.)

[2] Bennett Lerone, Jr., *Before the Mayflower*, Viking Penguin, 1993.

[3] *McCleskey v. Kemp*, 481 U.S. 279 (1987).

THE REV. JEW DON BONEY

THE CASE OF GARY GRAHAM

CONGRESSMAN MICKEY LELAND told me once: "Let's not talk about helping the many; if you can, help the one." In just ten days Gary Graham is scheduled to be executed on August 17th [1993].[1] He is an innocent man.

Gary Graham was convicted on the testimony of a single witness; an African-American testified that she saw Gary Graham commit a murder. The interesting thing about that is that there is absolutely no other evidence that ties him to the murder, so we have the testimony of a single person sentencing him to death row.[2]

Since that happened in 1981, we have since uncovered, by securing the district attorney's file and using our investigators, four crime scene witnesses who gave statements to the police at the time of the murder in 1981 who were never called to trial; two new crime scene witnesses who only came about several months ago; five alibi witnesses, all of whom have passed polygraph tests. And of those witnesses, only three have ever been heard in a court of law, only one ever testified at trial, and the others have not.[3]

In fact, we found that the evidence in the district attorney's files says that although the prosecutor put on a witness who said that the bullet that killed the victim came from a 22-calibre gun, and

---

REVEREND JEW DON BONEY An ordained Baptist Minister and civil and human rights activist, is Chairman of the Houston Chapter of the Black United Front. Reverend Boney organized and led the multi-racial coalition that was successful in freeing Clarence Lee Brandley from Texas' death row. A writer, leadership development trainer and community organizer, Reverend Boney has appeared on several national news programs.

that when Gary Graham was arrested he had a 22-calibre gun, and the jury heard that, they did not hear anything about the ballistics report that was in the police files that said the gun they retrieved from Gary Graham was not the gun that fired the fatal bullet.[4] The jury was misled.

We found the affidavit of Mervyn West, the trial investigator and a white former Houston Police Department officer, in which he explains that, "Because they [two contacts in the Houston Police Department] knew Gary was guilty of the other crimes, they thought that Gary was guilty of the murder... I, too, assumed that Gary was guilty."[5] There's no doubt that Gary Graham had committed other crimes, but there's equally no doubt that he's not guilty of the murder for which he has been sentenced to death. In the affidavit, Investigator West states that, as he assumed Gary Graham was guilty, "I decided not to waste time trying to substantiate his alibi."[6]

With all of that information available now, and virtually none of that being presented to a court of law, the State of Texas, the Supreme Court and the state courts have decided to execute Gary Graham without even giving him the benefit of an evidentiary hearing where all these witnesses can be heard in a court of law.[7]

What can we do about this? People say we're apathetic. But, no, it's not that we don't care. We're alienated, we're frustrated. And it seems that as much as we reach out, as many eloquent words as may be levelled, people simply just don't understand that it takes, as Dr. King said, suffering, struggle and sacrifice.

The question really is, how much are you willing to sacrifice? What price are you willing to pay? How much do you value the life of a human being? We all know and understand how much we

To the degree that we who carry the light of human consciousness and human rights devalue the lives of those we don't know, those who are far away, or those whose price we are not willing to pay as a sacrifice, is the degree that human life is devalued and the degree that the death penalty is allowed to grow and flourish and be maintained.

value our lives, or the lives of our families, or our brothers or our sisters; but when it's someone we don't know, when it's someone we have to go into our pockets to try to save, when it's someone who may not be of the same economic, cultural, social or political background, then somehow the degree of value and the degree of sacrifice we're willing to make tend to become less and less.

To the degree that we who carry the light of human consciousness and human rights devalue the lives of those we don't know, those who are far away, or those whose price we are not willing to pay as a sacrifice, is the degree that human life is devalued and the degree that the death penalty is allowed to grow and flourish and be maintained. So if we can't somehow find today a reason and a way to try to save Gary Graham's life, then why are we talking about abolishing the death penalty? Because the death penalty is about saving human lives that we can save and saving those who are before us now, not those who may be before us later.

What are we to do? Do we recognize the time and what must be done? Brothers and sisters, this is it. We are it. There's no one to turn to but us. We are the ones who have to take up the challenge or admit to ourselves that we're not up to the challenge and we're hypocrites, this is a hobby, this is an avocation, we're not seriously committed to abolition and we're not seriously committed to human rights. Or we have to take up the challenge and be willing to pay the price.

Something has got to be done. The times we live in and the challenges we face demand that we give and expect the very best of ourselves. Nothing less will do.

NOTES

[1] Gary Graham was not executed on August 17, 1993. At the time of publication, his execution was stayed pending the outcome of further litigation.
[2] Gary Graham Justice Coalition, *Update*, September 8, 1993.
[3] Ibid.
[4] Ibid.
[5] *Affidavit of Mervyn H. West*, In Re Gary Graham, State of Maryland, County of Howard, March 31, 1993, para. 5.
[6] Ibid., para. 11.
[7] Decision, Pete Lowry, District Judge, County of Travis, State of Texas, August 3, 1993.

STEPHEN B. BRIGHT

RACE, POVERTY AND DISADVANTAGE IN THE INFLICTION OF THE DEATH PENALTY IN THE DEATH BELT

RACE, poverty, disadvantage, politics and the passions of the moment determine who is sentenced to death in the "death belt," the states of the old Confederacy that historically have carried out most of the executions in the United States. Since the reinstatement of the death penalty in 1976,[1] those states have carried out almost 90 percent of the executions in the United States. Unfortunately, however, many of the states in other regions are becoming more like the South.

I was introduced to the quality of justice in capital cases in 1979, when I was practicing law in Washington, D.C., and someone asked me if I would take a look at a capital case from Georgia. Since at that time I was living in a place that did not have the death penalty, this was the first time I had examined a record in a death penalty case from the South. To this day I remain shocked by what I saw. The entire record in the case was only about an inch thick. That included everything—pretrial motions, jury selection, trial. Not much had occurred during the trial because the lawyer merely showed up. He didn't do much of anything. He presented no de-

STEPHEN B. BRIGHT Director, since 1982, Southern Center for Human Rights, Atlanta, Georgia; J. Skelly Wright Fellow in Public Interest Law at Yale Law School. Teaches courses at both Yale and Harvard Law Schools on the influence of race, poverty and disadvantage in the infliction of the death penalty. Has represented those facing the death penalty at trials, on appeals, and in post-conviction review proceedings. Author of, most recently, "Counsel for the Poor: The Death Sentence Not for the Worst Crime but for the Worst Lawyer," *The Yale Law Journal*, May 1994, Vol.103, no.7.

fense to the charges and nothing to explain why his client's life should be spared.

My shock was even greater a few weeks later when, for the first time, I met the man who was now my client. He was an 18-year-old African-American. I soon found he was suffering from schizophrenia, was not oriented as to the date, time, or place, and did not understand the legal proceedings that were going on around him. None of this appeared in the record of his case.[2]

In every state in the death belt where the death penalty is imposed—in Texas, in Mississippi, in Alabama, in Georgia—there are certain communities that are always sending people to death row. Many other parts of the state are not doing so at all. And we find in most of those states a lack of any kind of organized system for providing competent legal representation. The only southern state which is a deviation from this is Florida, which does have public defender programs, but even there the funding has been so far behind the need that often the public defenders do not handle many of the capital cases. In other states, local judges appoint anyone who is licensed to practice law, but those lawyers may not have any commitment to their clients, any understanding of the issues, or the experience required to defend a capital case.

I have seen four capital cases in Georgia in which the lawyers appointed by the judge referred to their own clients on the record by the slur, "nigger."

The criminal justice systems in this country are the institutions in our society that have been least affected by America's civil rights movement. As I go around the rural South today, I see that many institutions have changed, maybe not as much as they should have, but there are changes in the schools, changes in the hospitals, changes in the housing authorities. And yet when I go into the courtrooms of the South, I see that nothing has changed. Often the only minority person in the courtroom is the person on trial.

Today we still see all-white judges, all-white prosecutors, all-white defense lawyers and all-white juries deciding cases involving crimes against members of the minority community, and also involving members of the minority community who are accused of those crimes. In Columbus, Georgia, for example, 70 percent of the victims of crime are African-American; almost 90 percent of the people accused of crimes are African-American;[3] and yet, up until just a few years ago, not a single prosecutor was African-American.

In the 21 years that Georgia has had its new death penalty law on the books, the decision to seek the death penalty in Columbus has been made by a white man, the District Attorney.

Until recently, Georgia had only five African-American judges, four of whom were in Atlanta, and one in Augusta. As Governor of Georgia, Jimmy Carter appointed the first African-American judge in Columbus, but in the next election that judge was defeated by a white candidate, so his tenure as judge ended after only two years. In the South, judicial boundaries are drawn in a way to dilute the minority vote in order to keep minorities from becoming judges. And of course the judges are the people who appoint the lawyers for poor people who cannot afford counsel. Another reason for the absence of minority lawyers and judges in the South is the long history of race discrimination by law schools there. As a result, there are not many minority lawyers.

We did a study in Columbus, Georgia, which found that 70 percent of all victims of murders in that community were African-American.[4] When we looked at the cases for which a death penalty was sought, we saw that 80 percent of the murder victims were white.[5] That did not square up, so we started looking for the reasons. In one case we found that the father of a young white woman who had been killed was a wealthy contractor who had done work for the District Attorney. The District Attorney simply called him and asked, "Do you want the death penalty?" and the man said, "Yes, I do." And the District Attorney said, "That's all I need to know."[6]

The District Attorney sought and obtained the death penalty. When he ran for judge in the next election, the contractor contributed $5,000 to his campaign.[7] When the District Attorney's assistant, who had helped him handle the case, ran for District Attorney, the contractor donated $3,000 to his campaign,[8] and that assistant is today the elected District Attorney in Columbus, Georgia.

But when we went to the homes of African-American people in

that community who had lost a loved one—a wife, or a child, or a parent to murder—we found that the District Attorney had never called to ask them whether they wanted the death penalty. In fact, time after time, we found that nobody called them at all, not even to tell them that the case was in the court system or had been plea-bargained out to a manslaughter charge.

Repeatedly, we found that where the victim was the son or daughter of a prominent white family the District Attorney simply called a press conference and said, "The family wants the death penalty, and I'm going to get the death penalty." But in one case I had where the accused was a young African-American named William Brooks, that same prosecutor was not even aware that William Brooks' father had been murdered on the streets of Columbus, Georgia. He did not even know that the senior Mr. Brooks, a man who had served his country in the military, had been killed. He did not even know what had happened to the case.

We see racial discrimination in the criminal justice system that we would not tolerate in any other area of American life. In Jackson, Mississippi, Ed Peters, the elected District Attorney, says his policy of selecting a jury is to "get rid of" as many black people as possible.[9] What other public official could announce to the press that he was getting rid of people on the basis of their race? Yet, in sworn testimony, Ed Peters said that was the way he picks juries, and the courts held that it was all right. Leo Edwards was sentenced to death by an all-white jury and executed by the State of Mississippi, even though his jury was picked pursuant to this policy of getting rid of all African-Americans in the jury pool.

The South turned to perfunctory death penalty trials, where everybody knew before the trial started what the outcome would be, as a way around the bad press it was getting for lynching people.[10] These kinds of legal lynchings still take place in capital trials throughout the country today.

Poverty is another crucial factor that determines who receives the death penalty. The major consequence of poverty for those facing the death penalty is having a court-appointed lawyer. It is having a judge who may have made his or her way from district attorney to judge by discriminating, by seeking and using the death penalty as a political tool, and who is now the person who appoints the lawyer for the poor person accused of a death-eligible crime. Poor people accused of crimes do not pick their lawyers. They are stuck with their lawyers. But any mistake the lawyer makes is held against the person accused, not against the lawyer.[11]

I represented a man in Jackson, Mississippi, several years ago. After I had spent about 800 hours on his case, the city of Jackson paid me $1,000—a little less than $2 an hour. You cannot find many good lawyers for $2 an hour. In Alabama right now, the going rate to prepare for trial on a capital case is $20 an hour, with a cap of $2,000. If you spend 500 hours getting ready for trial, that means you get $4 an hour. A paralegal at a law firm in Atlanta who just fills out forms in bankruptcy cases is paid $75 an hour. I see death penalty case after death penalty case where the court reporter is paid more than the lawyer appointed to defend the accused.

In one of the cases handled by our office, a woman was sentenced to death in Talladega, Alabama, after her husband had abused her and the children for 15 years.[12] Halfway through, her trial had to be stopped because her lawyer had come to court that morning so intoxicated he could not go forward. The jury was given a day's recess. The lawyer was sent to jail, along with the client. The next morning both the lawyer and his client were produced from jail, and the trial resumed. A few days later the woman was sentenced to death. The woman's other court-appointed attorney was later disciplined by the Alabama Bar for neglect in two workmen's compensation cases, allowing the statute of limitation to run in both cases.[13] Thus, the woman was represented in a case in which her life was at stake by two attorneys, one intoxicated and the other incompetent to handle a workmen's compensation case. The trial judge, apparently unconcerned about such unconscionable representation before him, later appointed the lawyer who had been intoxicated during trial to represent the woman on appeal. However, our Center, upon being alerted to what had occurred, took over the appeal. Nevertheless, the Alabama Court of Criminal Appeals and the Alabama Supreme Court upheld her convictions and death sentence.[14]

In another case, John Young was sentenced to death in Georgia. He met his lawyer in jail shortly after his trial. It turned out the lawyer had been arrested and convicted of both state and federal narcotics charges. He said later that during the trial he had been on drugs; that he'd had a number of personal problems and had not been able to focus on the trial.[15]

This kind of lawyering does not mean these cases were set aside. John Young was executed. He is a dead man, despite the fact that he was represented by that lawyer. Billy Birt was represented by a lawyer who never challenged the under-representation of African-Americans on the jury.[16] Later, when the lawyer was asked to name all the criminal cases he was aware of, he could name only two—the *Miranda* Decision and the *Dred Scott* Decision.[17] The *Dred Scott* Decision is not a criminal case. That lawyer did not challenge the racial discrimination in the jury because he was totally ignorant of the law.

Numerous examples exist of capital cases handled by lawyers trying their first cases. One Mississippi man on trial for his life was defended by a third-year law student.[18] Cases abound where lawyers make basic mistakes due to ignorance, neglect or carelessness. Their clients pay with their lives, while another person, sometimes the co-defendant, whose lawyer did raise a challenge, gets a life sentence. If we just switch the lawyers, we would switch the results in those cases.[19]

Vengeance takes precedence over justice in many courts in the death belt. I was involved in a case in Georgia not long ago where a prosecutor had used all his jury strikes to strike all the African-Americans from jury service. Another prosecutor called him to the stand and asked his reasons for those strikes; and he claimed they had nothing to do with race, that it was just a coincidence that nine out of his ten jury strikes were used against African-Americans. He knew he was lying. I knew he was lying. The judge knew he was lying. Yet at the end of the process the judge said, "I find no race discrimination has gone on here." The people sitting in the audience, watching, knew this was not the truth. But there were political goals and goals of vengeance to be satisfied, quite apart from the interests of justice.

We are sentencing to death children, we are sentencing to death people who have suffered debilitating poverty and deprivation, we are sentencing to death people with mental retardation, and we are sentencing to death the mentally ill. The death penalty has become class warfare, being fought top-down against the poorest and the most powerless people in our society.

The execution of those with major mental illnesses, such as brain damage and schizophrenia, is unconscionable. In 1992, we saw an execution in Arkansas, over which the man who is now President of the United States presided as Governor, involving a young man named Ricky Rector who had a history of mental problems.[20] After he committed the crime for which he was sentenced to death, Ricky Rector put a gun to his head, pulled the trigger, and did serious damage to his own brain.

The very night he was executed, Mr. Rector, who had a habit of saving his dessert for later, had so little comprehension of what was happening to him that he told people he was going to vote for Bill Clinton for President. After he was executed, they found the dessert he had put aside, thinking he would have it later that evening after his execution. The notes of the guards who kept track of Ricky Rector's movements on death watch reflected he was howling like a dog, laughing uncontrollably, and had little or no comprehension of the fate that awaited him.

A few years ago, I represented a young man who was a military policeman in South Carolina.[21] He realized he was losing touch with reality and hearing voices nobody else heard. He went to the mental health facility at the base and pleaded for treatment because he knew something terrible was happening to him. Unfortunately, it was the Friday evening of the Christmas party, and he was told to come back on Monday. Over the weekend, the young man committed what all of us would agree were unspeakable acts, and ultimately he was executed by the State of South Carolina, despite his mental problems.

For a number of years, I represented a man who had been rejected from the military because of his mental illness. He had spent 30 years in various psychiatric facilities in the State of New Jersey. The final entry in his record read: "This man is extremely dangerous to himself and to others because of his mental illness. He should be committed to a mental institution." Instead, he was allowed to leave prison, stick out his thumb and hitchhike around the country. Ultimately, he killed two people and was sentenced to death in Mississippi.[22] Allowing this man on the streets without care and supervision was unfair to the victims of these crimes, to society and to the man himself.

We see case after case of people with severe mental illnesses being sentenced to death, not receiving the treatment they need before being released into the community. Why is this allowed to go on? One reason is that communities often are caught up in the passion of the moment. And particularly in cases involving the mentally ill, the crimes themselves may evoke such horror that insufficient attention is paid to the problems that provoked them.

Race, poverty and politics also come into play. Additionally, lawyers appointed to defend people with mental illnesses often lack the expertise to recognize their clients' problems. People are sentenced to death and later give up their appeals because they are severely depressed, or delusional, or are not in touch with reality.

Often juries sentence people to death without receiving any information about the person whose life is in their hands. Often the impairment is not apparent—such as brain damage, sometimes prenatal brain damage due to fetal alcohol syndrome. Robert Harris, who was executed in California, was a victim of fetal alcohol syndrome.[23] I represented a number of clients who were damaged before they were born because of the mother's abuse of liquor or drugs during pregnancy. Often lawyers who handle these cases are not aware of the warning signals of those kinds of problems or of the subtler signs of brain damage or of other injuries their clients might have.

Frequently, lawyers fail to have the investigators and social workers develop a social history which might signal these kinds of problems. Sometimes the lawyers never even obtain school or hospital records of their clients. In one case I had in Georgia involving a person with mental retardation, the only time my client's court-appointed lawyer had talked about him to the jury was when he called him "a little 138-pound nigger man."[24] If that lawyer had just looked at his school or military records, he would have seen that he represented a person who had an I.Q. in the low 60's, who could not make change, who could not drive a car, who was a profoundly disabled individual. But the jury never heard any of that because the lawyer had never investigated the case. The system cannot work when sentencers are deprived of such fundamental information.

And Americans must be reminded that they cannot remain smug and indifferent to human rights abuses at home as they deplore human rights abuses in other parts of the world.

We are sentencing to death children, we are sentencing to death people who have suffered debilitating poverty and deprivation, we are sentencing to death people with mental retardation, and we are sentencing to death the mentally ill. The death penalty has become class warfare, being fought top-down against the poorest and the most powerless people in our society. And there is little prospect for improvement. Instead, the situation I have described is deteriorating as a result of the expansion of the death penalty and the curtailment of careful review of death sentences by the courts in response to the demagoguery in the crime debate.

At this time, it is widely perceived by those in power that there is no constituency for fairness, for justice and for full enforcement of the Bill of Rights in our courts. How else can one explain the support for the death penalty or the silence regarding it by those who know that it is not working and that it has always been used against minorities and the poor? How else can one explain Bill Clinton's scheduling the execution of a brain-damaged man for the new Hampshire primary campaign and then making a show of returning home to preside over the execution?

Those who profess to be our leaders suggest that the Bill of Rights is nothing more than a collection of technicalities that stand in the way of effective law enforcement. Elected officials, judges and leaders of the legal profession remain indifferent to racial discrimination and inadequate representation of the poor in the criminal justice system. The pursuit of justice continues to lose out to the pursuit of vengeance.

The attention of the international community and those of conscience in this country is critical if this is to change. Americans need to be reminded of what Attorney General Robert Kennedy told the South in 1961, "If one person's rights are denied, the rights of all are endangered."[25] And Americans must be reminded that they cannot remain smug and indifferent to human rights abuses at home as they deplore human rights abuses in other parts of the world.

NOTES

1 *Gregg v. Georgia*, 428 U.S. 153.

2 Seven years later, the death sentence was set aside by the federal courts due to ineffective assistance of counsel. *Thomas v. Kemp*, 796 F.2d 1322 (11th Cir.), *cert.denied*, 479 U.S. 996 (1986). Although I have serious doubt about whether this young man was guilty of the offense charged, his conviction was upheld and he continues to serve a sentence of life imprisonment. I do not believe he would have been convicted of the crime if he had been adequately represented at trial. However, it is enormously difficult to prevail on a claim of ineffective assistance of counsel, no matter how deficient the representation provided to the accused. I have described the standard for ineffective assistance of counsel in "Counsel for the Poor: The Death Sentence Not for the Worst Crime but for the Worst Lawyer," 103 *Yale L.J.* 1835, (1994).

3 *State v. William A. Brooks*, Super. Ct. of Muscogee County, Ga. No. 5888, 54606, hearings of September 11-14, 1990. Information developed during the *Brooks* litigation was collected and published by the Death Penalty Information Center and the Southern Christian Leadership Conference in a booklet, "Chattahoochee Judicial District, The Buckle of the Death Belt; The Death Penalty in Microcosm," available from the Death Penalty Information Center, 1606 20th Street, N.W., Washington, D.C. 20009.

4 *State v. Brooks*, supra n. 3, Exhibit 1A.

5 Ibid.

6 Ibid., Exhibit 48 at 38 (testimony of James Isham).

7 Clinton Claybrook, "Slain girl's father top campaign contributor," *The Columbus Ledger-Enquirer*, Aug. 7, 1988, at B-1.

8 Ibid.

9 *Edwards v. Scroggy*, 849 F.2d 204, 207 (5th Cir. 1988), *cert. denied*, 489 U.S. 1059 (1989).

10 The relationship between lynching and the death penalty is described in Dan Carter, *Scottsboro: A Tragedy of the American South* (LSU Press, rev. ed. 1991); George Wright, *Racial Violence in Kentucky, 1865-1940: Lynchings, Mob Rule and "Legal Lynchings"* (LSU Press 1990). See also W. Witzhugh Brundage, *Lynchings in the New South* (U. Illinois Press, 1993).

11 Stephen B. Bright, "Death by Lottery—Procedural Bar of Constitutional Claims in Capital Cases Due to Inadequate Representation of Indigent Defendants," 92 *W. Va. L. Rev.* 679 (1990).

12 *Haney v. Alabama*, 603 So.2d 412, *cert. denied* (1992).

[13] "Disciplinary Report," *Ala. Lawyer*, November 1993, at 401.
[14] *Haney v. Alabama*, 603 So.2d 368 (Ala. Crim. App. 1991); *Ex parte Haney*, 603 So.2d 412 (Ala. 1992).
[15] Affidavit of Charles Marchman, Jr. at 1-5, *Young v. Kemp*, No.85-98-2-M.A.C. (M.D. Ga. 1985).
[16] Transcript of Hearing of April 25-27, 1988, at 231, *State v. Birt* (Super.Ct. Jefferson County, Ga. 1988).
[17] *Miranda v. Arizona*, 384 U.S. 436 (1966); *Dred Scott v. Stanford*, 60 U.S. (19 How.) 393 (1857).
[18] *State v. Leatherwood*, Miss. S. Ct. No. DP-70 (trial transcript).
[19] Examples are described in Bright, "Counsel for the Poor," supra n. 2, 103 *Yale L. J.*
[20] *Rector v. Arkansas*, 280 Ark. 385, 659 S.W.2d 168, *cert. denied*, 466 U.S. 988, 80 L.Ed.2d 842, 104 S.Ct. 2370 (1984). The circumstances surrounding the Rector execution are recounted by Marshal Frady, "Death in Arkansas," *New Yorker*, Feb. 22, 1993, at 105.
[21] *Shaw v. Martin*, 733 F.2d 304 (4th Cir. 1984).
[22] *Wheat v. Thigpen*, 793 F.2d 621 (5th Cir. 1986).
[23] *People v. Harris*, 28 Cal.3d 935, 623 P.2d 240, 171 *Cal. Rptr.* 679.
[24] Transcript of Opening and Closing Arguments at 39, *State v. Dungee*, Record Excerpts at 102, (11th Cir.) (No. 85-8202), decided sub mom. *Isaacs v. Kemp*, 778 F2d 1482 (11th Cir. 1985), *cert. denied*, 476 U.S. 1164 (1986).
[25] Edwin O. Gutman & C. Richard Allen, *RFK: Collected Speeches*, (Viking 1993), (Law Day speech at the University of Georgia Law School, Athens, Georgia, May 6, 1961).

YVONNE SWAN

NATIVE AMERICANS AND THE DEATH PENALTY

I AM A MEMBER of the Sinixt/Arrow Lakes Nation. My territory is in the land that is now occupied by the United States and Canada. My territory, mostly in Canada, is in what is now considered Southeast British Columbia. I was born and raised in Northeastern Washington State, lived on a reservation, pursued my education, and have worked off the reservation some years.

I am now the Coordinator of the Indigenous Prisoner Rights Project for the International Indian Treaty Council and its interim office director. I serve on the advisory board for Leonard Peltier, who is the number one prisoner of war in this country. I also work on behalf of Clifford Dan, of the Western Shoshone Nation, an elder who is also a prisoner of war.

I have firsthand experience in the court system as a defendant in the *State of Washington versus Yvonne Wanrow*. The case took 12 years from beginning to end. There were seven intense years of litigation. I was convicted by an all-white jury on Mother's Day, 1973, for shooting to death a child molester.

I won a new trial at the Supreme Court level of Washington State,

YVONNE SWAN Representative of the International Indian Treaty Council Information Office in San Francisco and Coordinator of the Prisoner Rights Project, also serves on the Advisory Board for Leonard Peltier's Defense Committee. Ms. Swan was a defendant in a murder case that set a legal standard for women's self-defense and defense of children, and has come to be known as the Wanrow Instruction. She participated in several European speaking tours supporting the Treaty Council delegation at the U.N. Commission on Human Rights in Geneva, and is the 1993 recipient of the American Indian Movement's Ruben Snake Memorial Leadership Award.

and "the Wanrow Decision" came out of that victory.[1] I am very happy, because all of those years were worth it, in the sense that the decision is now helping women.

What we Indian people have to go through is criminal. We have been in this country, on this land, since time immemorial.

I have worked with the court system on a tribal level on the Colville Reservation in Washington State. I studied as a paralegal, but because there was an issue in Canada whereby my ancestors' graves were being dug up and the burial remains stored in museums, I had to quit my job. I became involved with the American Indian Movement and the International Indian Treaty Council because I became aware of other instances where Indian people were run through the courts, found guilty, and imprisoned. I was one of the fortunate ones. I was not sent to prison. I did three days in jail. I was able to remain out on bond and play an active part in my defense. Many prisoners are not afforded that right. I guess the Great Spirit was with me, which is another issue that needs to come to the fore, because many of our people are denied the right to religious freedom on death row and in the prison system.

In this country there are two standards. One is ours as caretakers, and the other is the standard of the destroyers.

The death penalty was imposed on my people from the day that the colonizers first set foot on this land. Our nation, the Red Nation, one of the four sacred nations of the world, has been dying a slow death ever since. We are engaged in a war, an undeclared war waged against us by the United States and Canada. We are defending ourselves and at the same time trying to repair our nations. There are several nations in this country, and when I speak of international work, I am talking about the interrelationship, the political work, among indigenous sovereign nations of this country.

In this country there are two standards. One is ours as caretakers, and the other is the standard of the destroyers. I am learning a lot about languages and about other people; but based on tradition, which is what our people are trying to follow in this world today, we have our original duties and instructions to take care of this land, and that's all that we are trying to do. That's all we were doing the day the colonizers came here.

We don't believe in the death penalty. If we did, there wouldn't be any other people here but the indigenous peoples. We believe in sharing. We are a loving and peaceful people. In fact, we entered into agreements of peace and friendship with the United States—371 agreements—and all of them have been broken by the United States.

In those treaties we were guaranteed health, education and welfare. None of those guarantees is being upheld. Instead we are given crumbs for programs to help our people. But at the same time the war goes on, our people are being divided, assimilated, destroyed, diseased, imprisoned and murdered. If the history books were rewritten, there wouldn't be enough libraries to hold all these books, because they would contain obituaries of our people.

A descendant, a grandson of one of the 38 Dakota men hanged at Mankato not so long ago, refers to history as "his story," referring to the white man. Truth in history has to be brought out from the indigenous peoples.

In March 1993, an Indian man was executed in Delaware. His name was Red Dog. I would be interested in knowing about his background and his legal counseling, because I know, as a defendant, that there is very little justice. There is ineffective assistance of counsel on practically all levels. If you don't have the money, you might as well be looking toward life in prison or on death row.

When I look at U.S. history and U.S. government, I view it as the best that money can buy, because that's what it's based on—monetary and political gain. So, in reality, all of us, we who are powerless against the system, are political prisoners in my people's land.

Last week an Indian man was murdered before he was even brought to trial in Oklahoma. In the past year there have been four deaths of Indian people there—three in the prisons and one recently. Our people haven't even had a chance to get to trial. They are being murdered.

This man last week was beaten by the police. He was in custody for only two hours. His name was Marvin Hogner. He was 30. He was a father, a Cherokee in Adair County. Witnesses in the jail heard him say that he was going to sue the police for beating him. Later they found him hanged in his cell, and police said he hanged himself using the cord of a mattress.

Through our Board of Directors, I have become aware of three cases in Montana where white men were excused for being drunk during the commission of a crime while Indian people were condemned for that.

Statistics are recorded about our people, but I don't believe these statistics because many of them are recorded by people who do not understand that there are many Indian people, full-blood people, who are not enrolled in federally recognized tribes, so those people are not even counted. The statistics you get about the number of Indian people in prisons are much lower than the actual numbers.

I have gone into Montana State Prison as a spiritual adviser. I know that 30 percent of the people in that prison are Indian and it is like a warehouse. Two brothers, Lester and Vern Kills-On-Top, are on death row. During the time they were sentenced to death, a one-year-old Indian child was killed by a white woman. She sexually abused the child so severely it resulted in the child's death, and she was shown leniency, yet these two men were put on death row.

The white men used the sword and the rifle against us. They cannot totally annihilate us, so they use the pen to make laws to draw borders and boundaries around our land, and they use the bottle. Germ warfare has been going on for 500 years. Alcohol is another form of germ warfare. These are lethal weapons. The stereotyping, the hype, the naming of sports teams after Indians—Braves, Chiefs, Redskins—they all come into play here and lead directly to racism.

Chief Crazy Horse of the Oglala Sioux issued warnings against alcohol, yet there is now a Crazy Horse Malt Liquor for sale. People are

I would ask that people look into the history of colonialization in this country and see how racism, stereotyping and all other forms of death penalty against the Indian people are active today. This is not last year, or 20 years ago. This is today.

trying to get this taken off the shelves, but we're more or less helpless. The general public is being duped into thinking there are equality and human rights in this country and that there are no political prisoners.

I would say using the name of Chief Crazy Horse to sell liquor is pure racist hatred of Indian people. We are the only people who stand in the way of total land acquisition in this country. We have always stood in the way by reason of ownership, and we still stand in the way. This is like twisting the sword on Indian people to show their hatred for us and how they can deny our human rights and deny us respect. It's a slap in the face because there are descendants of Crazy Horse protesting this and they are not being heard.

Our people are afflicted with alcoholism, yet there are no really good treatments available to them. Many of our women give birth to children with fetal alcohol syndrome. They do not have a chance in the world. They are born with alcohol addiction, and they are sent out into society with no treatment. They don't have anywhere to go. Eventually, they are caught up in the spiral of violence and put on death row.

Alcohol is legal. It probably always will be legal because it's the biggest money-maker in this country. It's killing our people, and we are condemned for it. It's just another act of genocide perpetrated against our people.

It is very difficult during this war to try to repair our nations and assert our sovereign rights, protect our land and resources, and at the same time help our people and try to prevent them from getting caught up in the spiral of violence.

In my case I found that juries are selected by those who register to vote. Not many Indian people believe in this system because it is not our system but a foreign system imposed on us on our land. So, the chances of getting Indian people on a jury are very small.

I would ask that people look into the history of colonialization in this country and see how racism, stereotyping and all other forms of death penalty against the Indian people are active today. This is not last year, or 20 years ago. This is today.

NOTES

[1] *Washington v. Wanrow*, 88-Wn. 2d 221, 559 P. 2d 548.

SAFIYA BUKHARI-ALSTON

THE DEATH PENALTY IS A POLITICALLY REPRESSIVE TOOL

I AM A FORMER MEMBER of the Black Panther party and the Black Liberation Army. I came to death penalty work by way of my involvement in the liberation struggle for black people in this country. My being here is a result of work around the death penalty case of Mumia Abu-Jamal who is a former member of the Black Panther Party and a journalist and who is on death row in Pennsylvania.

Mumia Abu-Jamal is not the first political person or member of the Black Panther party who has been on death row. As recently as 1953 Ethel and Julius Rosenberg were executed because of their political beliefs and affiliations. The first member of the Black Panther Party to face the death penalty was Romaine "Chip" Fitzgerald, and he remained on death row in California until the death penalty was declared unconstitutional and a moratorium was placed on executions. If this had not happened, he would have been executed. In 1975, in the Commonwealth of Virginia, I faced the death penalty for 30 days (until it was declared unconstitutional in Virginia). Its constitutionality was subsequently reinstated, but

SAFIYA BUKHARI-ALSTON Director of Administration, Brooklyn Legal Services Corporation A, and Vice President and Minister of Defense of the Republic of New Afrika, is a former member of the Black Panther Party. In 1973, following a grand jury subpoena to testify about the Black Liberation Army, she went underground. Captured in Norfolk, VA, in 1975, she was given a trial which lasted a single day and was sentenced to 40 years in jail. Since her release on parole in 1983, Ms. Bukhari-Alston has devoted extensive time to support for political prisoners. She co-hosts a weekly WBAI-FM radio show, is the recipient of the 1971 Malcolm X Black Unity Award, the International Black Women's Congress 1990 Oni Award, and is the author of *Lest We Forget*, among other books.

By executing him the state will be sending the message around the world in cacophonic tones that if you want to live you have to be quiet and accept the racism, police terror, exploitation and injustice in this society. The alternative is death at the hand of the state apparatus. The death penalty is a tool of political repression.

during that short window of time I was tried and convicted without a death penalty threat over my head. When I ceased to face the death penalty, I still faced 900 years in prison. I ended up being sentenced to 40 years and spending eight years and eight months in prison because of my political beliefs and affiliations. If the death penalty had still been in effect, I would have ended up on death row. I was still in prison when they executed the first person in Virginia after 1976. Clearly, it was a means of making an example and instilling fear in the hearts of people.

The reason why members of the Black Panther party were and are on death row is because of the threat we pose to the system by our daring to speak out resoundingly against the oppressive nature of this system as it relates to people of color, particularly people of African descent. There was and is nothing that makes us different from anyone in this country other than the fact that we are and were political. If Mumia Abu-Jamal had not taken a political stand against police brutality and spoken out as a "voice of the voiceless" for people whose voices fell into a void and were lost in the abyss, and if Romaine "Chip" Fitzgerald had not been involved in political activities, they would not have come in contact with the judicial system. If I had not begun to do work around the issues of injustice, racial oppression and political exploitation in this country, I would not have been involved in anything that remotely dealt with the judicial system.

But, in speaking out against racism and class oppression in this society as it relates to people of color, we became targets of the criminal justice system and our political activity was criminalized. This criminalization of our political activity came from a desire to make people around the world believe there is no injustice in this country and, therefore, no reason for black people in this country to be involved in a struggle for liberation. Because of this struggle for Black liberation and the level of political education and awareness that was growing in the black community, it was necessary for the government to criminalize political activities in this country.

In criminalizing this political activity, they had to make people believe that we were in fact thugs and criminals involved in criminal activity. They then proceeded to treat and try political prisoners like criminals. Through their control of the media and the criminal justice system, they were able to convince people that we were criminals and they denied us the right to raise political issues and expose the political nature of what was happening to us. This, therefore, allowed things like the sentencing of Mumia Abu-Jamal to death and the other political lynchings of political prisoners in this country.

I'm not going to spend a lot of time talking about it, but I wanted to raise the issue of the death penalty in this country being a political tool to silence political dissent, and it didn't just start with the Black Panther Party. From the very beginning, as we go back to the history of slavery in this country, the history of slave rebellion in this country, the lynching of Nat Turner, when slaves rebelled as a result of racism, oppression and economic oppression, lynchings were used as a tool to silence dissent.

It is clear that fear is keeping people of color oppressed, telling them that they should not be struggling, that they should accept the status quo, that they should not stand up and demand their human rights. The Rosenbergs were executed as political prisoners in the 1950's. Now the sons of the Rosenbergs are standing up and saying, in the case of Mumia Abu-Jamal, that if we allow that execution to happen, we will be opening the gates to letting the United States Government know they can use the death penalty as a politically repressive tool.

Mumia Abu-Jamal, the present Black Panther facing execution in Pennsylvania, is known far and wide as the "Voice of the Voiceless." By executing him the state will be sending the message around the world in cacophonic tones that if you want to live you have to be quiet and accept the racism, police terror, exploitation and injustice in this society. The alternative is death at the hand of the state apparatus.

The death penalty is a tool of political repression.

MARIA ELENA CASTELLANOS

THE DEATH OF RAMON MONTOYA

THESE ARE the dying words of Ramon Montoya, a man who had never been convicted of a felony or of any serious crime before the occasion of the incident whereby he was charged with the murder of a Dallas policeman. In the final hour of his life, we discussed all the demonstrations, the hundreds of people who had taken to the streets of Reynosa, Tamaulipas, and in San Luis Potosi, Mexico, and had thereby delayed his execution in January of 1993.

I discussed with him a statement that had come from the Mexican Federal Congress earlier that day, addressed to the Governor of the State of Texas, requesting a stay of execution and requesting a beginning of negotiations between the Mexican government and the government of Texas and the United States Congress that would seek a humane solution to these ongoing executions. I read to him that statement and related to him the concern of thousands of people, nay, millions of people, throughout the United States and in Mexico about his execution.

I related to him a statement by Rigoberta Menchu Tum that also pleaded for clemency, and a statement sent to the Governor by 100 distinguished Latin American artists, intellectuals, writers, including Nobel Prize winners of literature, Octavio Paz and Gabriel Garcia Marquez, all of them seeking clemency, all of them asserting the

MARIA ELENA CASTELLANOS Criminal and civil lawyer practicing in the state of Texas since 1982; advisor and member of community defense committees for several death-row inmates, including Ricardo Aldape Guerra, Ramon Montoya, Leonel Herrera and Gary Graham; founding member of the Binational Network Against the Death Penalty (Mexico-USA).

"It doesn't matter," he said, "if you can't save me. It doesn't matter if the people cannot save me. They must continue to strive for justice with dedication and with strength."

right to life. After I read to him those statements and described to him the world outcry that was beginning to pour into the Governor's office, he said to me:

"No importa. Ha oido Ud. Lo que le hieierona Carlos Santana? No importa si no me puedan salvar a mi esta noche. No importa si el pueblo no me pueda salvar. Quiero que sigan luchando por la justicia con animo y con fuerza."

"Have you heard what they did to Carlos Santana?"

The State of Texas had executed Carlos Santana two days prior on March 23rd in Huntsville, Texas.

"Yes," I told him.

"It doesn't matter," he said, "if you can't save me. It doesn't matter if the people cannot save me. They must continue to strive for justice with dedication and with strength."

AUTHOR'S NOTE: Thousands of Mexican protesters received the body of Ramon Montoya on March 27, 1993, at the International Bridge between Hidalgo, Texas, and Reynosa, Tamaulipas, Mexico. Thousands more gave him a hero's burial in Reynosa the following day.

NEAL WALKER

EXECUTIVE CLEMENCY AND THE DEATH PENALTY

I AM AN ATTORNEY in New Orleans, Louisiana. I have been defending criminal cases in the South since 1979. Since 1985, my practice has been devoted exclusively to defending men and women charged with or convicted of capital crimes. I have also been involved in a number of clemency proceedings under two governors' regimes in the State of Louisiana.

There is no justice in the American system of capital punishment, and there is no mercy either. For, if mercy is the consideration that animates the exercise of executive clemency, we have seen precious little of it in the last 20 years. When it comes to the exercise of executive clemency, the quality of mercy is not simply strained but strangled. Clemency proceedings, when conducted at all, are often shams.

The case of Robyn Parks[1] in Oklahoma illustrates this. The five members of the board of pardons in Oklahoma first refused to give Robyn Parks a hearing on his claim. Finally, three of them voted to do so. Two of those later confessed they voted to conduct the hearing simply to expedite the execution. They thought if they didn't conduct the hearing, some judge would intervene.

In the case of Warren McCleskey[2], Mr. McCleskey was granted a hearing before the Georgia Board of Pardon and Paroles only after

NEAL WALKER Attorney in New Orleans, Louisiana, specializing in the defense of death-penalty prosecutions. He has defended scores of capital cases at all stages of the process, from trial through clemency proceedings. Former director, Kentucky Public Defender Capital Trial Unit. Recipient of 1991 National Legal Aid and Defender Association's Defender Services Award.

There is no justice in the American system of capital punishment, and there is no mercy either.... When it comes to the exercise of executive clemency, the quality of mercy is not simply strained but strangled.

the Attorney General of the State of Georgia promised to wage a full-scale campaign to overhaul the Board of Pardon and Paroles if they voted to commute the sentence of Warren McCleskey. Not surprisingly, even before the hearing was conducted, the chairman of the Board announced there would be no change in the sentence. McCleskey was executed.

The Harold Lamont (Wili) Otey case[3] from Nebraska also illustrates how these proceedings are often shams. Wili Otey had a hearing before a three-member Board which included the Attorney General of the State of Nebraska. The Attorney General, of course, had prosecuted him. His subordinates submitted the case on behalf of the State at the clemency proceeding. And, not surprisingly, Otey was denied executive clemency.

When Mr. Otey appealed to the Nebraska Supreme Court and claimed that he had not received a fair clemency proceeding and therefore had been denied due process of law, the Nebraska Supreme Court rejected his appeal.[4] This is a quote from the opinion which, in many ways, illustrates the prevailing state of the law with respect to executive clemency: "The exercise of executive clemency is a free gift from the supreme authority to be bestowed according to its own discretion."[5]

Now, that proposition of law was supported by a long list of citations to other court decisions, but the Supreme Court of Nebraska might just as well have cited a verse from the Book of Exodus: "I will show mercy on whom I will show mercy."[6] We see that the exercise of executive clemency has changed very little from ancient times.

There was a time in the history of the United States, from the 1940's to the 1960's, when the exercise of executive clemency was a fairly frequent occurrence. Throughout most of the 1940's, an estimated quarter of all death sentences were commuted by American governors.[7] As late as the 1960's, roughly one in every sixth capital sentence was commuted[8]. That statistic has now dwindled to something like one in 40, and it's still dropping.[9]

We have the benefit of some recent research by Professor Michael Radelet and Barbara Zsembik who have inventoried all the grants of executive clemency in the last 20 years. They have documented 70 cases since 1972, and we must add to that list a commutation from the State of Missouri in 1993.[10]

But that figure is unrepresentative, because 41 of those commutations were not traditional grants of clemency inasmuch as we think of clemency as a humanitarian act. Those 41 acts of clemency occurred in Virginia and Texas. In those states death sentences were commuted because the Supreme Court had invalidated death sentences in other cases, and it was clear that a number of prisoners had not received constitutional trials, and it was thought to be more expedient to simply commute the sentences rather than put the state to the expense of re-prosecuting. When you winnow out those cases, you end up with 30 grants of executive clemency.

Think about that. Close to 3,000 people on death row, well over 200 executions since 1977, and 30 grants of executive clemency.[11] Texas alone shows you how appallingly small that figure is, with 77 executions and no grants ever of executive clemency.[12] Also notably absent from the list of commutations in the last 20 years are: California, Arizona, Illinois, Oklahoma, among others—jurisdictions which have carried out executions and have more than 100 people on death row but no grants of executive clemency.[13]

We have some idea why those 30 people were commuted. Professor Radelet's research indicates that nine of them had their sentences commuted because of doubts about their guilt. Two of those came from Virginia. But we can't really talk about those Virginia commutations without also recognizing that Roger Keith Coleman[14] went to his death in Virginia with a very strong claim of innocence.

In the modern era, only eight prisoners have had their death sentences commuted because of mental illness.[15] This is shocking for two reasons. One is because of the super-concentration of mentally disabled offenders on death row. You might call it "disability row."

The other reason is that, historically, mental disabilities have been one of the chief reasons governors have commuted death sentences in this country. In fact, in California, mental disabilities were most frequently cited as the reason for granting executive clemency.[16]

Even Ronald Reagan, as Governor of California in 1967, granted clemency to a death-row inmate on the basis of mental disability. Reagan commuted the death sentence of Calvin Thomas[17] who had fire-bombed his girlfriend's home and killed her three-year-old son. Reading from the press release: "Clemency was granted because an EEG and psychiatric evaluation conducted after Thomas was convicted revealed preexisting brain damage resulting in a chronic mental condition."[18] Reagan emphasized that this information was not made available to the jury.

When Governor of New York, Nelson Rockefeller commuted the sentence of a youth named Salvatore Agron[19] due to massive evidence of an unstable homelife, mental retardation and a lengthy history of psychiatric institutionalizations.[20] Governor Rockefeller was incredulous that this evidence had not been presented to the jury.

Even in my state of Louisiana, in 1940, Governor Sam Jones commuted the death sentence of a prisoner named Jessie Lawrence James. The petition of the Lieutenant Governor and the Attorney General "appealed from a broad humanitarian consideration and from a medical point of view on behalf of an inmate who was described as below average intellectually, having the mental age of a normal child of six or seven years."[21]

The petition of the Lieutenant Governor stated: "Only after the trial and conviction did the sentencing judge have any knowledge of the degree of intelligence and competent mental age of the prisoner. On one occasion he was mentally unbalanced and treated for several months in the Central State Hospital at Pineville."[22]

We see that in the modern era virtually no prisoners have had their sentences commuted. I identified eight cases commuted because of mental illness. Six of those cases were commuted by Governor Richard Celeste in Ohio on his last day in office. Governor Celeste commuted a total of eight cases. His successor, Governor Moinavich, asked the Attorney General to litigate the legality of those commutations. Those cases are now pending in Ohio's Supreme Court.

Of the original inventory of 30 humanitarian commutations, a number came from the State of New Mexico. Five sentences were commuted by Governor Toney Anaya on his last day in office because he was opposed categorically to the death penalty.[23]

Scores of prisoners with mental disabilities have been executed in this country: Jerome Bowden,[24] with mental retardation, killed in Georgia, 1986; Johnny Garrett,[25] schizophrenic, killed in Texas, 1992; Robert Harris,[26] fetal alcohol syndrome, neurological dysfunction, killed in California, 1992; Larry Joe Johnson,[27] Vietnam veteran, suffered from post-traumatic stress disorder, executed in Florida, 1993; Ricky Ray Rector,[28] lobotomized, executed in Arkansas, 1992. And the case of Robert Sawyer[29] in Louisiana, 1993, in which I was involved.

Robert Sawyer's mother attempted to suffocate him with a pillowcase when he was an infant. Shortly thereafter, she committed suicide to escape the relentless abuse inflicted on her by her husband, Robert's father. As a teenager, Robert Sawyer had been institutionalized three times in mental hospitals, repeatedly diagnosed as having mental retardation and brain damage. The hospital records showed he had an abnormal EEG. The records also showed repeated prescriptions of anti-psychotic medication. The records showed electroconvulsive therapy as well. Yet Sawyer's court-appointed lawyer, who could have obtained these records with the ease of licking a postage stamp, presented none of this evidence to the jury and instead told the jury that his client was a sociopath.

We first presented this evidence in the fall of 1991 to a Louisiana Board of Pardon and Paroles under Governor Roemer's Administration. We convinced that Pardon Board that a commutation of Robert Sawyer's sentence was appropriate. The Board therefore recommended to the Governor that the sentence be commuted. We met with the Governor, and the Governor rejected the recommendation of his own Pardon Board. We received an eleventh-hour stay in the U.S. Supreme Court.[30] While the case was pending in that Court, Governor Roemer was defeated in his bid for reelection and Governor Edwards was elected.

After our appeal was dismissed by the United States Supreme Court, we had a different hearing in front of a different Board of Pardon and Paroles where we presented essentially the same evidence. Our case for clemency had improved by then. A juror from the original trial told the Pardon Board if he had known Robert Sawyer had mental retardation, he never would have voted to execute him. Yet Governor Edward's Board voted to deny clemency, and Robert Sawyer was executed. That's how arbitrary this process can be.

There is one bright spot in this bleak firmament, and that is the question of whether a convicted prisoner under sentence of death might be entitled to some degree of fairness in the commutation process. The traditional view is that the only clemency-related right enforceable in the courts is the right to apply for clemency. In other words, if a state extends the right of a condemned inmate to file an application for clemency, the state cannot unilaterally withdraw that right.

Why have we seen the decline of executive clemency in the modern era? I think the first reason is there is a perception, whether or not it is based in reality, that a governor who exercises executive clemency in a capital case commits political suicide.

Ironically, one of the most infamous Supreme Court death-penalty decisions of the modern era—the *Herrera* opinion—[31] contains the seeds of an argument that a condemned inmate might be entitled to some degree of due process. In this opinion, Chief Justice Rehnquist said: "Clemency is deeply rooted in our Anglo-American tradition of law and is an historic remedy for preventing miscarriages of justice where the judicial process has been exhausted."[32] Rehnquist described clemency as "the fail-safe in our criminal justice process."[33]

Two cases will tell us whether Chief Justice Rehnquist meant what he said and whether clemency will really be a fail-safe or whether it will continue to be the trap door it has been. One is the Otey case.[34] The Nebraska Supreme Court ruled that Mr. Otey's Pardon Board hearing, while possibly unfair, would not be revisited by the courts since clemency is an act of grace beyond the reach of the courts.

Surprising all of us in the legal community, Otey convinced the federal courts to grant him a stay of execution, and now the Eighth Circuit Federal Court of Appeals is grappling with the issue of whether the Due Process clause of the Federal Constitution entitles condemned inmates to some degree of fairness in these proceedings.[35]

The other case is Gary Graham's[36] in Texas. Gary Graham, like Leonel Herrera, has a very strong claim of innocence. The courts have refused to reopen the courthouse doors. To date, Mr. Graham has not been able to have a forum to present that evidence, although a trial court has ruled that he has a right to a hearing in front of the Board of Pardon and Paroles. Keep in mind that the Board of Pardon and Paroles earlier had refused to extend a hearing to Mr. Graham. But a courageous judge in Texas now has ordered the Board to conduct a hearing. I quote from his opinion: "My ruling in this case is based upon the Herrera court's assertion that the Texas clemency process is the fail-safe that prevents the execution of an innocent person."[37] So we can see that he relied on Chief Justice Rehnquist's opinion in the *Herrera* decision.

Why have we seen the decline of executive clemency in the modern era? I think the first reason is there is a perception, whether or not it is based in reality, that a governor who exercises executive clemency in a capital case commits political suicide.

Worse, I think there is a perception among some American governors that demonstrated enthusiasm for executions will ensure reelection or election to higher office. In Louisiana, for instance, when Governor Roemer was campaigning for reelection, television ads boasted that he had presided over the execution of five prisoners. "Five vicious murderers have been put to death because Buddy Roemer is willing to do more than just talk about capital punishment," the ads blared. Roemer was involved in a tight three-way race against former

Governor Edwards and former Nazi sympathizer and former Klansman, David Duke. David Duke's response to that ad was, "Only five?"

Governor Roemer didn't make it into the run-off; Duke and Edwards survived. But even as a lame duck governor, Roemer nonetheless tried to use Robert Sawyer's execution in a naked attempt to reelect his Lieutenant Governor. To enhance his Lieutenant Governor's reelection prospects, Governor Roemer gave him partial credit for his decision to deny clemency for Sawyer, raising the question of how many politicians can throw the switch at one time.[38] Both Governor Roemer and his Lieutenant Governor were defeated for reelection.

The central problem in this whole process, in my view, is incompetent trial counsel. Everything flows from that. Mentally disabled prisoners are sentenced to death because their trial lawyers didn't identify their disabilities. Innocent prisoners are sentenced to death because their lawyers failed to conduct thorough investigations. Often, the most compelling evidence in the case is not presented until the clemency stage. So even though, in theory, these death sentences are reviewed a number of times by both state and federal courts, in reality these reviews are based on inadequate evidence.

Imagine the unfairness that exists in the trials of people charged with misdemeanors and non-capital felonies, if it exists in the trials of people charged with capital crimes.

NOTES

1 *Parks v. Oklahoma*, 651 P.2d 686, *cert. denied*, 459 U.S. 1155, 74 L.Ed.2d 1003, 103 S.Ct. 800 (1983).

2 *McCleskey v. Kemp*, 481 U.S. 279 (1987).

3 *State v. Otey*, 205 Neb.90, 287 N.W.2d 36, *cert. denied*, 446 U.S. 988, L.Ed.2D 846, 100 S.Ct. 2974 (1980).

4 *Otey v. State*, 240 Neb. 813, 485 N.W. 2d 155 (1992).

5 Ibid. Harold Lamont (Wili) Otey was executed by the State of Nebraska on September 2, 1994. This was Nebraska's first execution in 35 years.

6 Exodus 33:19.

7 Hugo Adam Bedau, "The Decline of Executive Clemency in Capital Cases," *18 N.Y.U. Rev. of Law & Social Change 255*, 262.

8 Ibid., 263.

9 Ibid.

10 Michael L. Radelet, and Barbara A. Zsembik, "Executive Clemencies in Post-*Furman* Capital Cases", *Univ. Richmond LRev.*, vol. 27, 1993, 289-314. On June 3, 1993, Governor Mel Carnahan of Missouri commuted to life without parole the death sentence of Bobby Lewis Shaw. Mr. Shaw, who is mentally ill and has mental retardation, had been on death

row since 1980. On January 14, 1994, in one of his last acts before leaving office, Governor L. Douglas Wilder of Virginia commuted to life with the possibility of parole the death sentence of Earl Washington, Jr. Mr. Washington had been convicted of murder and rape but DNA testing showed he could not have been the rapist.

[11] NAACP Legal Defense and Educational Fund, Inc., *Death Row U.S.A.* (Winter, 1993).

[12] Amnesty International, United States of America, "Open Letter to the President on the Death Penalty," January, 1994, p.18.

[13] Radelet, supra.

[14] *Coleman v. Virginia*, 266 Va. 31, 307 S.E.2d 864, *cert. denied*, 465 U.S. 1109, 80 L.Ed.2d 145, 104 S.Ct. 1617 (1984).

[15] Radelet, supra.

[16] Note, Abramowitz and Paget, "Executive Clemency in Capital Cases," 39 *NYU L Rev.* 136, 146 (1964).

[17] *People v. Thomas*, 65 Cal.2d 698, 423 P.2d 233, 56 Cal.Rptr. 305, *cert. denied*, 389 U.S. 868, 19 L.Ed.2d 143, 88 S.Ct. 140 (1967).

[18] Office of the Governor's Press Release, 6/29/67; *Los Angeles Times*, Part 1, page 3, 6/30/67.

[19] *People v. Agron*, 10 NY2d 130, 176 N.E.2d 556, 218 N.Y.S.2d 625, *cert. denied*, 368 U.S. 922, 7 L.Ed.2d 136, 82 S.Ct. 245 (1961).

[20] Supra, note 16, pp. 166-67.

[21] *Application of Jessie Lawrence James for Commutation of Sentence From Death to Life Imprisonment in the State Penitentiary*, No. 10648, submitted by Lieutenant Governor and First Assistant Attorney General to Governor Sam Jones (1940).

[22] Ibid.

[23] *N.Y. Times*, November 28, 1986, at A 18, col. 1.

[24] *Bowden v. Georgia*, 239 Ga. 821, 283 S.E.2d 905, *cert. denied*, 435 U.S. 937, 55 L.Ed. 2d 533, 98 S.Ct. 1513 (1978).

[25] *Dallas Morning News*, 2/6/92, 20B.

[26] *People v. Harris*, 28 Cal.3d 935, 623 P.2d 240, 171 Cal.Rptr. 679.

[27] *Johnson v. Singletary*, 612 So.2d 575, 18 Fla. Law W.S. 90.

[28] *Rector v. State*, 280 Ark. 385, 659 S.W.2d 168, *cert. denied*, 466 U.S. 988, 80 L.Ed.2d 842, 104 S.Ct. 2370 (1984).

[29] *State v. Sawyer*, 422 So. 2d. 1136, *cert. denied*, 466 U.S. 931, 80 L.Ed.2d 191, 104 S.Ct. 1719 (1984).

[30] *Sawyer v. Whitley*, 945 F.2d 812, *cert. granted*, 116 L.Ed.2d 453, 112 S.Ct. 434, 60 U.S.L.W. 3374 (U.S. 1991).

[31] *Herrera v. Collins*, 113 S. Ct. 853, 122 L.Ed2/203, (1993).

[32] Ibid.

[33] Ibid.

[34] Supra, note 5.

[35] *Otey v. Hopkin*, 972, F.2/210 (8th Cir. 1992).

[36] *Graham v. Collins*, 896 F.2d 896, *reh'g granted, en banc*, 903 F.2d 1014 (5th Cir. Tex. 1990).

[37] Ibid.

[38] A New Orleans publication referred to this as "shameless political hay-making." *Gambit*, 12/16/91, p.14.

SONIA JACOBS

A SURVIVOR'S TALE

MY NAME is Sonia Jacobs. I am called "Sunny." I am a death row survivor. I was on death row for five years and in prison for sixteen years, 233 days. It took all that time for the truth to come out and for me to be free because I was innocent of the crime for which I was convicted and sentenced to death.

The way an innocent person is convicted and sentenced to death is one of the most confusing parts about the death penalty in the U.S.A. As a criminal defendant, I became a symbol for the legal system. Once you become a criminal defendant, all the wheels of the legal process are set in motion to convict you. The truth somehow gets lost in the process. It becomes irrelevant. No one in my case was looking for the truth. The defense attorney, hopefully, is trying to get you off, but is not necessarily looking for the truth. The prosecutor is trying to get a conviction, but is not looking for the truth. No one is looking for the truth. It is very sad. Once the wheels begin to grind, justice, too, becomes a victim.

Seventeen years ago, there were no women on death row at all in this country as a result of the decision that halted the use of the death penalty in this country for a period of time. So, when I got into this situation, there were no facilities for me.

SONIA JACOBS spent five years on Florida's death row and 16 years in the general prison population. Her conviction was overturned and she was released on October 9, 1992. Ms. Jacobs, presently Director of Development/Producer for Pro Bono Productions, an independent production company based in Los Angeles, is co-producer of "Justice On Trial: The Case of Gary Graham." She has taught yoga and delivered lectures on the death penalty and other human rights violations.

I was totally isolated on death row....You are totally stripped of your dignity. Your identity is taken from you. Inmate, inmate, that's all you are. So what happens is you reach down and you find an identity not only that you never knew existed, but that no one can take away from you.

I am not quite sure where I should begin the story of what happened. When this all began, I was a mother; I was a wife; and I was a daughter. By the time it was over, I was a grandmother. My children were grown, and I no longer could nurture them. I was an orphan because my parents had died. None of these things can be replaced.

My husband also was involved in the series of events that led to my incarceration for almost seventeen years. He was not as fortunate as I. He was executed. You may have heard of that particular execution because he was electrocuted by the State of Florida in what they called a "botched execution." His head caught fire, and smoke and flames came out of it. He was innocent. In the same month my husband was executed, a childhood friend came back into my life, realized my plight, and spent two and a half years fighting the system in order to free me, which is the reason I am here today. It took a miracle. That's the saddest part of all. There are others of us as well. I think of us as the phoenix people because we rose again out of the ashes.

What happens when you go to death row? The dehumanizing process begins in the jail. They let you know in no uncertain terms that you are not entitled to anything. You have rights; but if you exercise your rights, you will be punished. You plea-bargain. That is the most insidious invention in the legal process. What happens is the most guilty party is offered a plea bargain because he/she is the most likely to take it. An innocent person is not going to plea-bargain. The theory of being innocent until proven guilty does not work. You must prove your innocence. Of course, if you have never been through the legal process, you don't know this. So, when your attorney, who is being paid very minimally because she/he is an appointed attorney, has to defend you, you don't have the investigative powers the state has. You don't have the team of legal minds the prosecution has.

There is a "show" part to it. We did have a defense attorney, but it was a show. It's strictly a show. It's not effective. It can't be effective. I was not a castaway person. I had a family, but my family couldn't afford to pay six figures to an attorney. Therefore, I had to accept an appointed attorney. He did an adequate job, as far as fulfilling the obligation of giving me a defense, but it was not an effective defense. It couldn't be an effective defense because we had no way to refute the expert testimony. We had no way to dig into the discovery process. In my particular case, the prosecutor used coerced testimony, false testimony. This testimony was used intentionally. This was prosecutorial misconduct, a phrase I didn't know until later when I was able to get hold of law books and see what exactly had happened to me in that courtroom.

Falsified evidence and uncorroborated statements were used. Exculpatory evidence remained hidden until many, many years later. Testimony of a co-defendant was bargained for and used. My husband and I had a co-defendant who immediately pled to three life sentences and then testified against us. Later on, he confessed. They would not hear his confession. We found, accidentally, that his polygraph test was hidden from us. This polygraph test and an exculpatory statement made by the co-defendant which proved that I had done nothing and that my husband had done nothing, were all hidden. Years later, when I was on death row, I discovered it myself and brought it to my attorney's attention. We had a hearing. It was considered harmless error—harmless error that evidence showing our innocence was withheld.

Death row has a very special effect. I am beginning to wonder, now that I have met other survivors of death row, if the fact that we were innocent perhaps gave us greater strength. I suspect that it did. What happens on death row, especially for a woman, is that you can't spend your life nurturing, at least that's how we are taught. I got my greatest pleasure from taking care of my children, my husband, and even the thought of taking care of my parents when they got older, which I will never be able to do.

I was totally isolated on death row. For five years of my life, I spoke to no one. There was no one around except for a guard who came every hour, 24 hours a day, every day of my life, for five years. Every hour of my life for that time someone came, looked, and wrote down what I was doing.

You are totally stripped of your dignity. Your identity is taken from you. Inmate, inmate, that's all you are. So what happens is you reach down inside yourself and you find an identity not only that you never knew existed, but that no one can take away from you.

WALTER MCMILLIAN

STATEMENT TO THE UNITED STATES SENATE JUDICIARY COMMITTEE
APRIL 1, 1993

MY NAME is Walter McMillian. I was sentenced to die in the electric chair and spent nearly six years on Death Row in Alabama awaiting execution for a murder that I did not commit, a murder that I knew nothing about, a murder that I had nothing to do with. Today, the State of Alabama has acknowledged that I am an innocent man and that I was wrongfully convicted. What happened to me could have happened to you, or to anyone else. I was convicted and sentenced to death on the false testimony of one man. I am here today to urge you to do all that is in your power to prevent what happened to me from happening to anyone else.

I am now 51 years old. When I was arrested, back in June 1987, I had my own pulp-wood business. Pulp-wood is big in Monroe County, Alabama. In fact it may be the leading industry in the region, and what it involves is cutting down the pine trees and getting the wood to the paper mills. I had worked hard all my life. I had dropped out of school when I was a young boy and started working for my mother when I was only ten years old, plowing fields. As a young man, I had worked for a logging company, running a saw. In the early 1960's, when I was about twenty, I started my own pulp-wood business—by agreement, I would chop your pine trees down, cut them up and haul them to a wood yard, so that they could be shipped to paper

---

WALTER MCMILLIAN Fifty-two-year-old pulp-wood worker in Monroeville, Alabama. Charged with capital murder in 1987 for the shooting death of a young white woman in Monroe County, Mr. McMillian spent six years on Alabama's death row for a crime he did not commit. He was released in March of 1993.

I was sentenced to die in the electric chair and spent nearly six years on Death Row in Alabama awaiting execution for a murder that I did not commit, a murder that I knew nothing about, a murder that I had nothing to do with.

mills. Gradually, I came to own a couple of pulp-wood trucks, power-saws, and a tractor. Along with my crew of three to four men, we would cut any man's pine, regardless of the terrain.

I also raised three beautiful children—Jackie, Johnny, and James—with my wife, Mini. Jackie now lives up in Huntsville, and works for the State of Alabama. My two sons are still in Monroeville, and one of my sons, Johnny, has three beautiful children of his own. My uncles and aunts, my sisters and nephews and nieces, and of course my grandchildren, all lived near my family in Monroeville and shared with us many wonderful moments of celebration and happiness. We had a big family and many friends and lived our lives in a close community.

That's what we were doing on the morning of November 1, 1986—the morning that a young white lady, that I did not know, was tragically murdered at the Jackson Cleaners in Monroeville. At the time she was murdered, I was helping out at a fish-fry that my sister, Evelyne Smith, had organized to raise money for her church. A fish-fry is where you all get together and fry fish and sell the fish to raise money for your church. My sister Evelyne was the minister of her church. This fish-fry was taking place at my house, which is several miles outside of Monroeville in a rural area near Repton, Alabama. That morning, I was also helping my friend, Jimmy Hunter, a mechanic, who was working on my pick-up truck in my back yard. The transmission of my truck had been leaking, so Jimmy and I took the transmission out and we put in a new seal.

I learned about the tragic murder of that young lady, Ronda Morrison, when someone came by my house and told Jimmy Hunter and me that she had been killed earlier that morning in downtown Monroeville. We were all so upset about crime in our community. It was a shock for all of us. Six months went by and I did not hear much about the tragic incident at the cleaners. I had heard that there was big reward money, something like $15,000, for information leading to the arrest of the person that committed that crime. But that's about all I heard until June 7, 1987, the day I was arrested.

That was a Sunday. It was about 11:00 in the morning, and I was driving my truck down Route 84, a straight shot to my house, when all of a sudden I was surrounded by the police. There were cars of every type—State Troopers, city cars, the Sheriff and his deputies. They were everywhere, all behind me, on the side, and they stopped me right in the middle of the road. They jumped out with all kinds of guns, rifles, pistols, shotguns, and shoved me up against my truck. They yelled at me to put my hands over my head, not to ask any questions and not to look back.

This had never happened to me before and it was extremely terrifying. I don't know whether you've ever looked straight into the barrel of a shotgun, a rifle or a pistol, but I can tell you, it is a very frightening experience. Particularly when you are a black man in Southern Alabama. They told me to shut up and not say anything or else they would blow my brains out. I kept asking, "why are you doing me like this, what's going on?" And all they would tell me is that I was charged with sodomy. I asked them what that meant. And someone responded in a loud angry voice—and in vulgar terms—that I had sexually assaulted a man. I didn't even know what sodomy meant, and to this day I cannot understand why they arrested me on that charge. They never told me where, when or how I had committed this crime. It was simply a way to make me seem really evil and dangerous and a way to get my truck. The charge was later dismissed by the Court because there was no factual basis.

They put me in a State Trooper car and took me to jail. They took my truck to the station and kept it there. At the station, a jailhouse snitch named Bill Hooks examined my truck and later testified at trial that he had seen my low-rider near the cleaners on the morning of the crime. A low-rider truck is a pick-up truck that has been altered to ride low to the ground. But I had only had my truck converted to a low-rider five months *after* the incident at the cleaners, in May 1987. Because I had my truck converted to a low-rider *after* this murder, there was no way that anyone could have seen *my* low-rider truck near the cleaners on November 1, 1986, the day that young girl was murdered.

Within a couple of weeks, I was transferred to death row at Holman Prison in Atmore, Alabama—a State correctional facility. There, on death row, I awaited my trial for about one year. No one on death row, no one at the prison, no attorney I have ever spoken with—*no one* has ever heard of a capital defendant being placed on death row prior to trial and prior to being sentenced to death in Alabama. The reason is that the confinement on death row is the most restrictive confinement in the entire State and is not suited to a person that needs to communicate frequently with his lawyers and prepare for trial. To this day, I do not know why I was placed on death row one year before my trial.

Death row was a terrible experience. With the exception of forty-five minutes per day of exercise time and a few rare hours per week in the day room, my days were spent in my cell—twenty-three hours a day. My cell, a mere five-by-eight foot space, was my only world. Had it not been for the loving visits of my family and grandchildren, I may not have survived the experience. And even with their support, my experience on death row was traumatic.

I was wrenched from my family, from my children, from my grandchildren, from my friends, from my work that I loved, and was placed in an isolation cell, the size of a shoe-box, with no sun light, no companionship, and no work for nearly six years. Every minute of every day, I knew I was innocent. My family and friends knew I was innocent, and we all knew I had been wrongfully convicted for a crime that I had nothing to do with.

I have spent many hours—too many hours—trying to figure out why I was chosen to be the victim of this terrible injustice. I had no prior felony convictions and had not had difficulties with the law. I had worked hard all my life and had no debts. I had a family and friends and no one that I would consider my enemy. But I had made one mistake. One big mistake in Monroeville, Alabama. I had been seeing a white woman. And my son, he, too, had made one, terrible mistake. He had married a white woman.

The woman I had been seeing was named Karen Kelly. She was acquainted with this white man, Ralph Myers, who pled guilty to the brutal murder of another young woman that occurred at about the same time as the Ronda Morrison killing. Ralph Myers was the man that testified falsely against me.

My trial was a two-day nightmare. I don't know if you can understand how painful it is to have to sit quietly and watch, and say nothing, when people you don't know are taking an oath before God, making up lies as fast as they can speak, and accusing you of killing an innocent, 18-year-old girl in the prime of her life. I have a daughter, a beautiful, loving daughter that I cherish. How could I be accused of killing a young woman the same age as my own daughter? How could I have done that? What business would I have had, a black man known by all—black and white—in Monroeville, to walk into the cleaners in downtown Monroeville, steal money and kill an innocent person? I had my own business, my own trucks, my family and friends, my life. What on earth would have been my motive to do this?

I couldn't say a word as these people took the witness stand and lied about my whereabouts, and lied about my low-rider truck—that wasn't even a low-rider at the time of the crime—and lied about my doing something I would never do. Never. Something I had no business doing. It was agonizing to hear the lies and to sit there, watching.

But nothing was more painful than when the jury returned with a guilty verdict. We had put on a half-dozen friends and family members that had been to the fish-fry. They had seen me there all morning. They knew I couldn't have done this. They all testified that they had seen me and been with me all morning. But no one believed them. Fine, upstanding members of the black community—they were no match for a white, convicted felon. Ralph Myers, a self-proclaimed murderer, had more credibility to my nearly all-white jury than the upstanding members of our community who had gathered together to raise money for their church. The verdict was a hurting thing. It was especially traumatic for my family. They had seen me all that morning. They knew I was innocent. The verdict to them meant that they were liars, that they were worthless. If they had not known for sure that I was innocent, then maybe they could have speculated whether I had committed the crime. But there was no speculation for my family and friends. They all knew what the justice system had just done. They understood that we were all being punished.

What followed were another four-and-a-half years on death row. While I was on death row, I saw seven other prisoners executed. I experienced the executions with the greatest pain and with enormous fear about whether this would happen to me. From my cell you could smell the stench of burning flesh. The smell of someone you know burning to death is the most painful and nauseating experience on this earth.

What followed were also four-and-a-half years of hope and of prayers. I knew I was innocent and I knew that some day the truth would come out. I knew that some day my innocence would be proved. I had faith in the Lord. I had unwavering faith in the Lord. For nearly six years I prayed that that some-day would not come *after* my execution.

There are many things that concern me as I sit here today. I am excited and happier than I can describe to be free. At times, I feel like flying. However, I am also deeply troubled by the way the criminal system treated me and the difficulty I had in proving my innocence. I am also worried about others. I believe there are other people under sentence of death who, like me, are not guilty.

When you are poor and under sentence of death you worry about a lot of things. One of the biggest worries is whether you'll get the kind of legal assistance you need to save you from execution. I feel like I was very fortunate, but a lot of others have not been so fortunate and for many death-row inmates, it takes years to

---

I have learned more knowledge about human existence in these last six years than I would ever have desired. And I would like to share just one thing with you. Justice is forever shattered when we kill an innocent man.

---

get the kind of legal representation and investigation necessary to prove their innocence. If federal courts do not permit death-row prisoners to prove their innocence, even after many years on death row, and prevent wrongful executions, the hope of many innocent people on death row will be crushed.

It is important that you understand how important hope is to condemned prisoners. I have survived these six long years, but I am a different man. I have suffered pain, agony, loss, and fear in degrees that I had never imagined possible. My life will never be the same now. That is something I have come to terms with. I have learned more knowledge about human existence in these last six years than I would ever have desired. And I would like to share just one thing with you. Justice is forever shattered when we kill an innocent man.

DONALD CABANA

THE EXECUTIONER'S PERSPECTIVE

I SUPPOSE every camp has its clandestine enemy or adversary, depending on one's perception. I suppose I constitute that role because I am the executioner. I am probably the only witness to this Tribunal who has suffered the anguish and torture of carrying out the execution of other human beings.

I wish to address you concerning the execution process and the impact of the death penalty on the prison staff who are involved in executions. Fortunately, I am one of a very small brotherhood. There are probably a dozen other people in the United States who, like me, since 1976 have been called upon to carry out the supposed mandate of the American people to execute convicted felons.

Something has happened in the United States in the field of penology during the last several decades. In the 1930's, executions in this country were at their peak, and we were executing 150 to 200 or more people a year. During that time, Luis Laws, one of the most famous penologists in American history and warden at Sing Sing Prison in New York, and his famous colleague, Clinton Duffy, who served in the same capacity at San Quentin, executed over 500 men and women between them. Yet, during that same time, these men were outspoken critics of the death penalty. They were able to be out-

DONALD A. CABANA Instructor of Corrections, Department of Criminal Justice at the University of Southern Mississippi. Former warden, Mississippi State Penitentiary (1987-92, 1984-86). Former Commissioner, Mississippi Department of Corrections (1986-87). Served as a registered consultant for: the American Correctional Association (1982-92), and the HBO documentary "Fourteen Days in May" (1987).

spoken and critical because they were insulated from politics. Today, however, you find wardens who may very well express their opinions, as I have, upon retirement. However, the warden who dares to express opposition to the death penalty when called upon to carry it out will soon be looking for employment elsewhere.

In 1969, when I began my career in corrections, I think most of us in the field were convinced that, as our careers progressed and we got into executive positions, we would never have to face the terrible question of carrying out the death penalty. By 1969, this country had had an *ex officio* moratorium on executions for some two years. In 1972, with the *Furman v. Georgia*[1] decision, those of us in corrections were firmly convinced we would never again be called upon by the American public and the judiciary to carry out this awful penalty.

My career, during the next few years after 1969, carried me to Mississippi and then to Florida. In 1976, the Supreme Court did a complete U-turn.[2] When John Spenkelink was executed in Florida while I was in the penal system there,[3] I recognized for the first time that the stark reality existed that at some point I might very well be a warden in a death-penalty state and would be asked to carry out an execution. Spenkelink's execution, after all, was a landmark. It was the first execution in some 20 years in Florida. The distinguishing feature of the Spenkelink execution was his involuntariness, of course. He fought the process. He exhausted his appeals. He did not give way to the process and give the State of Florida a free ticket, as Gilmore had done in Utah.[4]

In a sense, Gary Gilmore's execution was treated by many of us in corrections as a surrealistic aberration. We still did not accept the reality that the death penalty was back in our midst. Gilmore's execution didn't convince us because he had obliged the process willingly. He had asked the State of Utah to do what he could not do personally, and the State of Utah was manipulated by Mr. Gilmore into committing suicide for him. When John Spenkelink was executed, I and many others in corrections instinctively knew that some of us eventually in our careers would not escape this scourge.

By 1984, I had left the State of Florida, made a stop for a few years in the Missouri State Penitentiary, and then returned to Mississippi as the warden of the Mississippi State Penitentiary at Parchmont. It was at Parchmont that my career in corrections and the death penalty collided head on.

Part of the difficulty for those of us in corrections who are called upon to carry out this most heinous of punishments is that we are taught, despite the picture often painted by Hollywood prototypes, to care about our charges. We are taught to believe—and you have to believe it if you're going to spend a career in corrections—that people can and do change. Then, all of a sudden one day you're told to kill somebody. And those two perspectives are diametrically opposed. You find yourself in the midst of a terrible clash of wills. Somehow, when the Attorney General of Mississippi called me early one spring morning in 1987, and said, "We're going to have an execution in just a few weeks," even after mulling it over, I did not believe it would happen. I did not believe it would happen until I gave the order to drop the lever and poison the man to death in the gas chamber.[5]

I recall, as my wife and I attended a private mass in the prison chapel earlier in the afternoon, even then I did not believe it. When an officer interrupted me during that service to hand me a faxed message from the U.S. Supreme Court, denying Edward Earl Johnson a last stay of his execution, I understood for the first time in my life, despite the fact that I had been born and raised in a very traditional Catholic family and educated in Catholic schools, I understood for the first time in my life those words that were spoken in the New Testament, "If it is your will, please, God, let this cup pass from my hands." I understood those words as I had never understood or appreciated them before.

The first time I had to execute a prisoner, however, I continued to indulge in self-denial right up until 12:01 a.m. I didn't believe it would happen, and I know he did not either. I still recall it—because technically in our ritualistic process, the execution cannot proceed until the executioner receives a final telephone call from the Attorney General and Governor, telling him that all obstacles have been cleared. When that telephone rings, you see, it has a far different sound for the prisoner who is strapped in the chair than it does for the warden. Our eyes locked on each other, and all I could do was shake my head, indicating that the execution would proceed.

Now, in the process of executing prisoners, I committed the cardinal sin for wardens: I became close to one of my death-row prisoners. There was something genuinely likable about Connie Ray Evans[6] and, for some odd reason, he took a liking to me. We just seemed to hit it off. For five of his seven-and-a-half years on death row, I was his warden. We talked every week, sometimes several times a week, and if, on rare occasions, I missed seeing him and talking to him, he would be sure to good-naturedly chastise me.

I watched this young man go through significant changes. We almost never mentioned the possibility that he might some day be placed in the gas chamber and executed. And yet I wished so many times that the process allowed the warden the power to commute this young man's sentence to life.

The day I received a telephone call from the Attorney General, telling me that Connie's execution would occur within the next few weeks, I was numbed, even though it wasn't the first execution I had faced. I found myself delaying that inevitable walk from my office to his cell to tell him the awful news that an execution date had been set. I did not want to make that walk.

But when I finally did, we talked for three-and-a-half hours, and over the course of the next six weeks, we spent many, many hours talking about everything, mostly about life, but increasingly, unfortunately, about the reality that was hurtling towards both of us.

This young black man arrived on death row as an 18-year-old who was embittered, a drug addict, and feeling sorry for himself. The young man I was going to be asked to execute was so very different. He was at peace with himself, he was at peace with the world, and he was at peace with his God.

...when we execute a human being, what we are acknowledging is that we have failed to find even a shred of redeeming quality to that person's life.

The remarkable thing about Connie Ray Evans is that he never once in all the years I knew him denied responsibility for his crime. He had a remarkable sense of faith. He was different from any prisoner I ever worked with during my 20-year career. He gave tremendous evidence of possessing many redeeming traits. And he was the classic example of why we should not execute people, if for no other reason than when we execute a human being, what we are acknowledging is that we have failed to find even a shred of redeeming quality to that person's life. And Connie Ray Evans offered so much more than a shred. He simply hoped that society would deem him worthy of a second chance.

Connie Ray Evans did not ask for freedom; he was a pragmatist above all things. He understood that he bore responsibility for what he did, and he also understood that at that point in his life, from his perspective, he did not have a right to ask society to live among free people again on the streets. But he did ask for a second chance at life. He was convinced that he had positive attributes to offer and contributions to make even from within the walls of a prison. He hoped for that miracle, but obviously the miracle never came.

The night before the execution, Connie and I sat in his cell all night, talking. By this time the pressure, the emotion, and the crush of events had stripped away the veneer of titles, roles and stations in life. I was not a warden to him any more than Connie Ray Evans was an inmate to me. We were, to put it simply, two human beings caught up in a vortex of emotions that neither of us could control and that neither of us could avoid.

To be sure, not all reminders of where we were could be done away with. There were still the steel bars and the loud noises and the electric locks and the sliding cell doors and the red jumpsuits that death-row prisoners are required to wear. But in spite of everything, Connie and I had reached a point in our travels together where, again, it was no longer a warden and his death-row prisoner, but just two people, caught up in legal maneuvering and the glare of publicity, who were really seeking privacy to simply enjoy life as two people ought to be able to do.

He thanked me for being a friend, and so many times I felt so awkward having him tell me what a friend I had been. He told me how he wished it could have been under other circumstances. He began to ask questions those last 24 hours about how things would go. He talked openly for the first time of his impending death, resigned finally to his fate. It was I who kept trying to find ways to bolster him, even though I knew in my heart there was no chance that this execution would be avoided.

And then, remarkably, during those last 24 hours, he said to me: "In my religion, I've been taught that when you die, if your reward is to go to heaven, any unanswered questions, any mysteries about life that you never understood, my God will answer my questions. And in that respect, I am looking forward to this coming to a closure, because I've been tortured for seven-and-a-half years wanting to know why I did what I did. And so in that respect, you see, you will be doing me a great service." How do you respond to a statement like that from a man who knows his appointed hour of death?

He talked about his family and his growing-up years, and with tears filling his eyes, he asked me about my family, my children, and my own childhood. And I was flooded with thoughts of how very different one can feel and yet how very close one can be. There is such a thin line between the keeper and the kept.

I was adopted at the age of nine by a loving, nurturing family. My mother was a prostitute who walked the very streets of this city [Boston], a heroin addict who ended up serving time in prison. My father was an alcoholic who sexually abused all of his children, including his sons. And the only mystery that I have ever found about people who end up on death row with histories of child abuse and neglect is not that they got there, but that it took them as long as it did. For each generation of abused children, we turn out the next generation of "monsters" who end up on death row or in psychiatric care for the rest of their lives.

It was Connie Ray Evans who was consoling me, and I thought I would die inside when he told me that he looked at the final hours of his life as a journey to a new and better existence, and that he was glad that I would be there with him to the very end.

The final day of Connie's life was the most difficult of mine. Privately, I kept hoping he would receive a stay or clemency from the Governor, though the practical side of me knew otherwise. As I observed my officers, those poor, beat-upon, negatively imaged people who form the backbone of a correctional institution, I watched the stress and the terrible pain of guards who had worked for eight years with this young man and who would turn their face from you, not in shame, but because they didn't want you to see the emotion and the pain and the burden on them. I could see the stress and pressure that was bearing down on all of them, because Connie Ray Evans by then was no longer an inmate to them either; he was a man who was as well-liked by the prison staff as he was by the other inmates.

At 11:15 on the night of his execution, 45 minutes before the appointed time, I had to go to Connie Evans' cell and tell him it was time to go to the last night room next to the gas chamber. Those words proved to be the single most difficult group of words I had ever spoken, even though I had spoken them before. He exchanged goodbyes with other inmates and staff. And then for the last 45 minutes of his life, he was alone with his chaplain, his warden and his God.

About five minutes before I was to walk him to the gas chamber, he noted how ironic it was that he should be executed at midnight, and he inquired as to why the state always chooses to hide executions at the dark hour. We had no secrets from each other, so I explained to him why the state executes people at midnight: In case there's a last-minute stay, the state still has 24 hours to rush through legal maneuvers and try to do the deed before midnight of the next day.

I suppose I would have reacted to that quite differently from Connie, but Connie's response was, "How ironic for the state, they think they're killing me at midnight, but for me it's a new beginning, a midnight sunrise on the rest of my life rather than an end."

He smiled at me and asked if it would be embarrassing or against prison rules for the warden to allow an inmate to hug him goodbye. As we embraced, I thought how sad that it takes a tragedy such as an execution to bring two ordinary human beings together. And then, in a whisper, he told me to be brave and that it was okay.

Seconds later, as I watched him being strapped into the cold, black metal chair inside the gas chamber, I realized for the first time that

I had been privileged to be witness to some of God's finest work. In fact, it was so good I realized in my own mind that if you were not a believer you could hardly come out of that execution chamber the same person.

I had watched a human being change before my eyes over the course of five years, a person who had become a different and far better person, in many respects far better than me or than many people I knew. I had watched Connie Ray Evans travel the long journey from an embittered, wretched, tortured soul to a man who was at peace with everything in his world. Always full of surprises, he saved his most important one for last.

The execution process is very ritualistic. I read the death warrant to him, telling him what he already knew, and then I asked the ritualistic question: "Do you have a last statement?" He said yes, but it was a private one that he wished to share with me alone. And as I bent down so he could whisper in my ear, he said, with tears streaming down both cheeks, "I don't wish to embarrass you, but from one Christian to another, I love you."

The executioner understands more than most the terrible need to find alternatives and solutions.

For a second, but what seemed to me at that time an eternity, I was speechless. What in the world could I possibly say to a person who had just told me he loved me, knowing I was about to snuff out his life?

I remembered thinking in a swell of emotions just for a moment that I could make the decision to walk away from this and not carry out this deed. And I know many of you will take issue with this rationalization. But, frankly, I called upon my faith one more time for two reasons: one, because Connie wanted me there, if it had to happen; and, two, because from my perspective, my God had a reason for my involvement, if it was nothing more than the fact, however minuscule, that I could carry a man to his death with some sense of dignity and compassion and humanity.

As I touched his arm, I told Connie that I loved him, too, and so did God. And in the final exchange of jocularity, with a sense of seriousness on the side, I said, "When you get to where you're going, I wish you'd put in a good word for me."

This is a long journey that I've chosen to share with you, and I hope it has given you a sense of the impact the execution process has on the people who are asked to do it. It is a journey, frankly, that, much like my experiences as a veteran of the Vietnam conflict, I have never returned from and probably never will.

In a very real sense, what I wish to leave you with is something that only a warden and his death-row prisoner can really experience. And that is, there is a bonding that occurs between the executioner and his charge that no one else can ever fully appreciate or experience. The executioner dies along with his prisoner.

The executioner understands more than most the terrible need to find alternatives and solutions. When Connie Ray Evans told me to be brave, I wish I could have found the courage to speak out with the force of a warden on this issue rather than waiting to find the courage of my convictions after I had retired.

But I choose not to dwell on what I might have done or what I could have said, but rather, on what I can contribute to the future. In that sense, I hope this message has in some small way brought renewed meaning to the death penalty debate and the efforts of Amnesty International and other organizations to end capital retribution in the United States.

And so the message from me to you, and from my friend Connie Ray Evans, is: No more killing. No more killing. Please, God, no more killing.

NOTES

[1] 408 U.S. 238.
[2] *Gregg v. Georgia*, 428 U.S. 153.
[3] Executed 05/25/79 (FL).
[4] Executed 01/17/77 (UT).
[5] Edward Earl Johnson. Direct Appeal Opinion: 416 So. 2d 389 (Miss. 1982). Executed 05/20/87 (MS).
[6] Connie Ray Evans. Direct Appeal Opinion: 422 So. 2d 737 (Miss. 1982). Executed 07/08/87 (MS).

LLOYD BARNETT

RESERVATIONS TO INTERNATIONAL DOCUMENTS CONCERNING THE DEATH PENALTY

THE INTERNATIONAL, customary and conventional law on the death penalty has reached a state of development where we can conclude that the death penalty is inhuman and degrading. It is the antithesis of the right to life. It denies the dignity of the human being.

In international conventions and in constitutions which deal with inhumane treatment, reservations or exceptions are made in favor of the preservation of the death penalty where it exists in particular countries. That seems to me to be an international concession that the death penalty offends the principle of respect for human rights.

The provisions which are usually found are, firstly, for the existing application to be maintained or to be preserved from the condemnation of the human rights declaration. Secondly, no further extensions should be made to the application of the death penalty. Thirdly, countries undertake to move aggressively toward its elimination. So the human rights norm condemns the death penalty, although it condones a measure of restriction on the application of international human rights law.

Whether or not the American reservation to the International Covenant on Civil and Political Rights[1] is valid or not is not a ques-

LLOYD GEORGE BARNETT LL.M., Ph.D., President, Jamaican Bar Association, 1976-1977, and again 1991 to present; Attorney-at-law, Jamaica, since 1960; Chairman, Caribbean Council of Legal Education, 1977-1983; President, Organization of Commonwealth Caribbean Bar Associations, 1984-1993; Member, Jamaican Bar Council, General Legal Council, and Rules Committee of the Supreme Court, 1967 to present; Author, *The Jamaican Constitution, Basic Facts and Documents*, 1992; *The Constitutional Law of Jamaica* (O.U.P.), 1977.

tion which we are going to determine now. But the application of the death penalty in the United States is in violation of certain principles, principles which are not the subject of reservations. Those are the principles of fairness in the application of penalties, fairness in the conduct of trials. These are key principles which are applicable and which are binding on the United States.

The judicial process in the United States is, at all levels, subject to competitive electoral practices and politics. Because of that, decisions as to who is prosecuting, decisions as to what charges are made, decisions as to which counsel represent the accused, decisions as to the jurors who sit on the cases, decisions as to the penalty which is imposed, decisions as to whether commutation of the death penalty is granted or not, throughout the judicial processes, those decisions are influenced by political party considerations. That clearly is an indicator of a potential conflict, if not an actual conflict, with the rule of law and the principles of justice.

There is a very grave and real risk that innocent people will be convicted and sentenced to death. The Supreme Court of the United States has held that the discovery of evidence subsequent to the condemnation which points to the possible innocence of the condemned person is irrelevant to the legal decision.[2] While that Supreme Court ruling stands, there is a very grave extension to the risk of innocent persons being executed.

Evidence shows that the death penalty is ineffective as a deterrent. At the Amnesty International Commission of Inquiry into the Death Penalty in the United States, relatives and friends of victims indicated that they do not demand retribution. There is no evidence of any national imperative that the death penalty should be imposed. There is also evidence that there are alternative methods which the public may be willing to accept of dealing with persons who are convicted of murder.

There is *prima facie* evidence in support of the view that the death penalty as it is practiced in the United States offends international law.

There is *prima facie* evidence in support of the view that the death penalty as it is practiced in the United States offends international law. The death penalty in the U.S. should be suspended immediately in the face of all this evidence.

NOTES

[1] Multilateral Treaties, Reservations, Understandings, and Declarations, deposited with the Secretary General, status of December 31, 1992, st/leg/ser.e/11, page 132.
[2] *Herrera v. Collins*, U.S. Supreme Court, decided January 25, 1993.

ROGER HOOD

THE INJUSTICE OF THE DEATH PENALTY

THE QUESTION these hearings have addressed is whether the imposition of the death penalty in the United States fundamentally violates human rights and is inevitably unjust, despite safeguards built into some state legislation designed to prevent unjustness.

Coming from Great Britain, which has such close ties to the United States, I am reminded of the democratic values we share, as well as our common language. We have admired the United States Constitution. The first modern states to abolish capital punishment were American—Michigan in 1846 followed soon afterwards by Wisconsin and Rhode Island. Therefore, to those who admire the U.S., it is disconcerting and deeply troubling to find, both at the federal level and in the majority of the states, so much resistance to the international trend which moves apace towards the abolition of the death penalty worldwide.[1] So strong is this resistance that in 1989 the United States voted against the adoption of the Second Optional Protocol to the International Covenant on Civil and Political Rights Aiming at the Abolition of the Death Penalty—along with Iran, Iraq, China, and several other countries which the U.S. has indicted for violation of human rights.[2] When the American government ratified the Covenant in 1992, it specifically en-

ROGER HOOD Director of the Centre for Criminological Research; Fellow of All Souls College, Oxford University. Former distinguished Visiting Professor at the University of Virginia Law School. Fellow of the British Academy. Author of: *The Death Penalty: A World Wide Perspective* (1989); *Race and Sentencing* (1992). Presented "The Death Penalty in International Perspective" to the Amnesty International Seminar on the Death Penalty CSCE Parallel Conference in Moscow, 1991.

...to those who admire the U.S., it is disconcerting and deeply troubling to find, both at the federal level and in the majority of the states, so much resistance to the international trend which moves apace towards the abolition of the death penalty worldwide.

tered a reservation in relation to the section calling for the abolition of the death penalty for those under the age of 18.[3]

The evidence we have heard before this Amnesty International Commission of Inquiry into the Death Penalty in the United States suggests that the U.S. is in breach of several of the nine safeguards adopted by resolution of the Economic and Social Council of the United Nations in 1984,[4] not only in relation to imposing the death penalty on juveniles and the mentally disordered, but also with regard to the standard which is set to ensure that capital punishment may be imposed "...only when the guilt of the person charged is based upon clear and convincing evidence leaving no room for an alternative explanation of the facts."[5] The evidence we heard gave cause for concern that this safeguard has been violated on a number of occasions, due largely to the very poor quality of defense attorneys available to indigent defendants, and the political influences which enter into the decision whether or not to charge defendants with capital murder. On all these grounds, Amnesty International's inquiry provided convincing evidence that the death penalty in America violates international standards of human rights and justice.

By executing offenders, the U.S. stands out among all those countries which regard themselves as liberal democracies which respect human rights. A mere glance at the list of countries where executions have been carried out, shows that they are, almost without exception, countries which have been criticized for their violation of human rights by the U.S. One wonders, therefore, how the federal and state governments can reconcile their place among nations which execute their citizens with their claims to be upholders of human rights.

The question that has to be raised, of course, is why there is so much support for capital punishment in the United States. It has not always been so. We know that in the mid 1960's, only 38 percent of the public were definitely in favor of the death penalty.[6] By 1991, 76 percent were in favor.[7] It seems to me that this is a reflection of the shift in political philosophy and in penal philosophy which has occurred in the U.S. over the last twenty years. It also reflects a change in what is expected from criminal justice. The system has become far more concerned with crime control, with much less emphasis being placed on due process and the rehabilitation of offenders. We have witnessed the development of punitive policies based on just deserts, deterrence, and incapacitation which have produced a dramatic growth in the population of prisons and jails in the U.S. By 1993, over 1,390,000 people were in custody.[8] It is hardly surprising that such a punitive climate also fuels strong support for the death penalty.

Yet, despite a disturbing increase in the number of executions in the United States in recent years, there are still few in relation to the total number of homicides. Rather than being an effective measure of crime control, executions serve merely a horrifying symbolic function. Indeed, the review of the literature on deterrence which I carried out for the United Nations convinced me that the claim that the death penalty has a unique deterrent effect cannot be sustained. One has only to examine the statistics to realize that the probability of execution for a homicide is so low in the U.S. that it could not have other than a symbolic purpose. The probability of being executed for a culpable homicide is, at the most, one in one thousand.[9] Even among those cases which are statutorily "death eligible," only about one in ten defendants is sentenced to death, and in only a fraction of those cases is the defendant actually executed.[10] Not only is execution unlikely to be seen as a credible threat by those who may be

...the death penalty cannot escape being barbarous, whatever attempts may be made to sanitize the infliction of death.

about to kill, it also makes it far more difficult to prosecute murder effectively and to ensure that adequate punishments are imposed.

There is also the belief—upheld by the U.S. Supreme Court in *Gregg v. Georgia*[11]—that the death penalty can be made acceptable so long as there is a narrow legal definition of capital murder. The aim is to eliminate arbitrariness and discrimination while at the same time limiting executions to the most egregious murders and the most dangerous killers. But the Royal Commission on Capital Punishment, in my own country, which reported forty years ago, came to the conclusion that:

> *It is impractical to frame a statutory definition of murder which would effectively limit the scope of capital punishment and would not have overriding disadvantages in other respects.*[12]

The evidence we have heard before Amnesty International's Commission of Inquiry bears this out and not only in relation to racial discrimination. A disturbing degree of arbitrariness, while less than in the past, still produces an unacceptable lottery.

It is also claimed that, through lengthy procedures of review and the use of clemency, the system of criminal justice in the United States eventually rectifies any wrongful convictions, so that no innocent persons need fear execution. The evidence presented to Amnesty International's Commission of Inquiry suggests that this is certainly not so. Finally, it is sometimes claimed that the death penalty can be made socially valuable by controlling crime, by reducing fear of crime, and by reaffirming the value of life through the maxim that those who take life must expect to have it taken from them. But as the famous philosopher of the Enlightenment, Beccaria, said in 1764:

> *The death penalty cannot be useful because of the example of barbarity it gives men...It seems to me absurd that the laws, which are expressions of the public will, which detest and punish homicide, should themselves commit it.*[13]

All of the evidence heard by Amnesty's Inquiry supports this contention that the death penalty cannot escape being barbarous, whatever attempts may be made to sanitize the infliction of death. There are the awful excursions to and from the death chamber and executions very many years after sentence has been passed. The case of William Andrews, who was recently executed seventeen-and-a-half years after he entered death row at age 20, is deeply shocking. In my country it would, I believe, be regarded as inconceivable that a 20-year-old should be executed after so long a period in prison. It is much more likely that he would have re-entered society, having been effectively rehabilitated by that time.

This Commission of Inquiry heard no testimony from those who support the retention of the death penalty in America and, therefore, cannot be said to have constituted a thorough and impartial inquiry into all the allegations made by witnesses. Nevertheless, no one who heard such powerful testimony could doubt that a strong *prima facie* case for the abolition of capital punishment was fully made.

A system of criminal justice can only be effective if it is perceived as legitimate and fair both by offenders and citizens in general. Ultimately, capital punishment, which cannot be inflicted fairly or without violating human rights, must undermine confidence in the criminal justice system rather than be supportive of it.

NOTES

[1] See Roger Hood, *The Death Penalty: A World-Wide Perspective* (A Report to the United Nations Committee on Crime Prevention and Control), Oxford University Press, 1989. The preface to the fourth impression of this study (1994) notes that, whereas over the 23 years 1965-1987, 25 countries and territories abolished the death penalty, 18 did so between 1988 and 1993.

[2] General Assembly Resolution 44/128. See William A. Schabas, *The Abolition of the Death Penalty in International Law*, Cambridge, Grotius Press, 1993, p.170. Fn. 230 lists the other countries who voted with the United States.

[3] Indeed, although the U.S. specifically mentioned crimes committed by persons under the age of 18, it reserved, in general, the right to impose capital punishment, subject only to the constitutional constraints imposed by the Supreme Court. See Schabas, Ibid., pp.92-3.

[4] Adopted by the U.N. Economic and Social Council in Resolution 1984/50.

[5] Ibid.

[6] Louis Harris, *The Harris Survey*, *Chicago Tribune*, Feb.7, 1977, reproduced in Nicolette Parisi et al., *Sourcebook of Criminal Justice Statistics: 1978*, U.S. Department of Justice, 1979, p.326, Table 2.65.

[7] George Gallup Jr., *The Gallup Poll Monthly*, No.309, June 1991. Reprinted in Kathleen Maguire et al., *Sourcebook of Criminal Justice Statistics: 1992*, U.S. Department of Justice, Washington D.C., 1993, p.205, Table 2.54.

[8] See *Prisoners in 1993 Bulletin*, Bureau of Justice Statistics, Washington, D.C., 1994, which

gives the total number of federal and state prisoners on December 31, 1993 as 948,881. See also *Jail Inmates 1992*, Bureau of Justice Statistics, 1993, which gives the total number of jail inmates on June 30, 1992 as 444,584. Extrapolating on the last five years' experience, the total prison (975,000) and jail (490,000) populations in 1994 are likely to be 1,465,000.

9 See Hood, *The Death Penalty*, op. cit., p.121. In 1991 there were 24,700 murders and non-negligent manslaughters known to the police and between 1985 and 1993 an average of 20 executions a year.

10 Of cases of capital murder in the 75 largest U.S. counties in 1988, 12 percent of defendants were sentenced to death. See *Sourcebook of Criminal Justice Statistics: 1992*, op. cit., p.539, Table 5.72.

11 428 U.S. 153 (1976).

12 *Report of the Royal Commission on Capital Punishment, 1949-1953*, London, H.M.S.O. Cmnd. 8932, 1953, p.278. The Commission further concluded, "It is impracticable to find a satisfactory method of limiting the scope of capital punishment by dividing murder into degrees." See also Hood, *The Death Penalty*, op. cit., Chapter 5, pp.85-105.

13 Cesare Beccaria, *On Crimes and Punishment*, 1764, trans. Henry Paolucci (1963), p.50.

GITOBU IMANYARA

THE DEATH PENALTY IN THE LAND OF LIBERTY

MY EARLIEST KNOWLEDGE in Kenya of America was one of freedom, one of the rule of law, and one of an independent judiciary that not only works but gives real meaning to the theories I learned in law school about the Bill of Rights. Therefore, I expected that, after an examination of the working of the death penalty in the U.S., I, like your founding fathers, would be able to confirm as "self-evident the truth that all human beings are born and created equal." I came to the land of liberty with an open mind expecting that I would vindicate my faith in the American system of justice.

After having heard the testimony from experts and victims of injustice presented at the Amnesty International Commission of Inquiry into the Death Penalty in the United States, practically every conception of American justice that I had has been shattered. After hearing testimony from some 30 witnesses and submissions of counsel, I can only say that the things I am discovering about the American system have shocked me beyond belief.

I am not able to say or to see the reasons why these things have been going on for so long in the land that was founded on liberty, a land that is, on the basis of the evidence presented before the Commission, engaged in the continuing betrayal of those very basic prin-

GITOBU IMANYARA Kenyan human rights attorney; founder of the *Nairobi Law Monthly*; editor-in-chief, *Nairobi Weekly*. Recipient of: 1993 Democracy Award, presented by the National Endowment for Democracy; 1991 FIEJ Golden Pen of Freedom (Switzerland); 1991 Percy Qoboza Foreign Journalist Award (Washington); 1991 Louis M. Lyons Award; 1991 International Human Rights Law Group Human Rights Award (Washington); 1991 Liberal International Prize for Freedom.

After having heard the testimony from experts and victims of injustice presented at the Amnesty International Commission of Inquiry into the Death Penalty in the United States, practically every conception of American justice that I had has been shattered.

ciples of liberty. International human rights statutes were inspired by the Declaration of Independence and the American Constitution. The framers of the United Nations Universal Declaration of Human Rights included eminent and distinguished American citizens. Why, then, is there such a huge gap between what Americans hold as basic universal standards and their practice in their own land?

In the course of Amnesty International's Commission of Inquiry, we heard powerful and irrepressible voices of witnesses who suffered the imposition of the death penalty and who have been found to be innocent. These people offer the most compelling, the most real reason as to why the death penalty cannot be justified in any form. In their world and their experiences are contained the irrefutable proof of the utter inhumanity of the death penalty. All the safeguards that are designed to ensure that only the guilty are executed are shown to be incapable of ensuring such a result.

In the application of the death penalty, justice, too, becomes a victim. The insidiousness of plea-bargaining that may lead a victim to plead guilty to a crime never committed for fear of being killed, the inadequacy of the public defender system, the prosecutorial misconduct, and the overwhelming evidence in the form of facts and figures indicating that the victims of the death penalty are the black and the poor are proof that the death penalty is inherently unequal in its application; and yet all human beings are born equal.

I saw a T-shirt on which was engraved the following: "The Death Penalty," and below it, "Vengeance, not deterrence. Racially and economically biased. Does nothing for victims. Kills innocent people. Sanctions violence. Mocks justice and human rights."

Nothing, in my view, could better summarize my own conclusions that the death penalty has no place in the modern world.

ABDUL CARIMO MAHOMED ISSA

HUMAN RIGHTS AND THE DEATH PENALTY

THE HISTORY of the rights of the human person has been confused with humanity's struggle for the realization of its democratic desires. The struggle for citizenship, slave rebellions, the disputes between patrician and plebeian, the establishment of political constitutions, were always throughout time and history examples of the struggle against manifestations of absolute power, and struggles for the dignity of the human spirit and person.

The *Magna Carta* in England of the 13th century, the institution of *habeas corpus* and the Bill of Rights in the 18th century all had a bearing and a voice in the Declaration of Independence of the United States of America and in the Universal Declaration of the Rights of Man and of the Citizen, proclaimed at the advent of the French Revolution. In these documents, the "equality of all citizens under the law and the right of life and liberty" are expressly recognized.

The 20th century has seen, on different occasions, retreats in the struggle to protect human rights, so that the protection of these rights must be raised to the level of a universal responsibility, whose universality and indivisibility have been reaffirmed once again in the recent World Conference on Human Rights in Vienna, Austria.

In the same vein, the Universal Declaration of Human Rights,

ABDUL CARIMO MAHOMED ISSA Special Advisor to Ministry of Justice, Republic of Mozambique, has been World Bank Consultant for the Program of Decentralization of the Local Government, Ministry of State Administration; Director-General of the National Institute of Legal Assistance; Chief Justice of the Peoples Court of Maputo City; and Judge of the Common Court of Gaza Province.

The facts presented before Amnesty International's Commission of Inquiry have exposed the practice of the death penaly in the United States as a vivid example which all must learn to repudiate and reject.

proclaimed by the United Nations in 1948, constitutes a common ideal to be attained by all peoples and all nations concerning those rights."[1] The Universal Declaration of Human Rights recognizes the right of each person to life and categorically affirms that "no one should be submitted to torture or to cruel, inhuman, or unusual treatment."[2]

From that perspective, the death penalty undoubtedly constitutes a violation of these rights, to such an extent that the movement for its abolition cannot in any way be disassociated from the movement for the respect of human rights.

The facts presented before the Amnesty International Commission have transformed the practice of the death penalty in the United States into a vivid example which all must learn to repudiate and reject.

If this country which is so wealthy and so powerful, and which affirms itself to be the greatest democracy in the world, the seat of the most advanced technology on the planet, has shown itself capable of producing testimonies to which we have just been a witness, there is good reason to ask, what would be the application of the death penalty in a country such as mine, Mozambique, in which: a) democracy, far from being consolidated, is still very embryonic; b) there is a rate of illiteracy of more than 70 percent; c) per capita income is less than U.S. $80 dollars per year; d) more than 60 percent of the annual national operating budget is supported by foreign assistance.[3]

The Republic of Mozambique instituted the death penalty in 1979, ceased to enforce it in 1986, and finally abolished it in November 1990,[4] for the basic reason that it was recognized to be a violation of human rights, and because proof was not found that the death penalty was particularly efficacious as a deterrent to the practice of violent crime.

We have listened with special attention to the testimony of witnesses on events which have occurred in the United States of America. This testimony demonstrates without equivocation that, apart from the death penalty constituting inhuman, cruel, arbitrary and discriminatory punishment, a serious risk is created of executing innocent persons. Therefore, in the belief that Man is the product of the society in which he lives; in the belief that the rehabilitation and reeducation of Man is the only path to follow to create a society which will be more just, more humane and more deserving of itself; the death penalty as a punitive measure, for all the reasons heretofore expounded, constitutes an inhuman, cruel, arbitrary and discriminatory punishment, a violation of human rights and, as such, should be abolished.

NOTES

[1] *Universal Declaration of Human Rights*, G.A. Res. 217A (III) U.N. Doc. A/810.

[2] Ibid.

[3] *The World Almanac: 1994*, ed. Robert Farnighetti, Mahwah, NJ, Funk and Wagnalls Corp., 1993, p.791.

[4] *The Death Penalty List of Abolitionist and Retentionist Countries* (December 1993), Amnesty International, p.1.

FLORIZELLE O'CONNOR

THE NEED FOR EDUCATION

PHYSICIAN, heal thyself. I say this because I am from Jamaica where capital punishment is still in force. Physician, heal thyself. I say this to the citizens and government of the United States of America, the country which has carefully marketed itself as the liberator of the world, the holder of all principles which mirror the belief that all men are born equal.

The death penalty is efficient as an agent of social control. It is compatible with the doctrine of political expediency. It maintains the status quo, ensuring that minorities and the poor of whatever color know their place and have places reserved for them within prisons and ultimately on death rows whenever the state dictates.

Fundamental rights which we take for granted, even in an undeveloped country like Jamaica, and for the rest of the civilized world, such as the right to trial, the right to adequate legal representation, the right to appeal, have become virtually nonexistent in the U.S.

I would like to make two practical suggestions:

1. Serious efforts should be made to properly present and build on some of the evidence which was heard at the Amnesty International Commission of Inquiry into the Death Penalty in the United States, with a view to submitting it to the Rapporteur on Arbitrary Executions of the United Nations for investigation into these matters.

2. Since this evidence poses a challenge to all people of goodwill,

---

FLORIZELLE O'CONNOR is Co-ordinator for the Jamaica Council for Human Rights, Kingston, Jamaica, a position she has held for the past 14 years. Ms. O'Connor is also the Current Affairs presenter for radio and television news.

We must inform and educate the people of the United States about the absolute travesty, the absolute mockery the death penalty makes of all concepts of justice and decency accepted in the civilized world.

---

it must be used to educate the American people and their legislators. We face the tremendous task of starting virtually immediately a serious public education program aimed at all levels of American society. We must inform and educate the people of the United States about the absolute travesty, the absolute mockery the death penalty makes of all concepts of justice and decency accepted in the civilized world. Americans must begin to revitalize the principles of equality and justice on which their country was founded. If they don't begin this very difficult job, history will not absolve them.

BELISARIO DOS SANTOS

THE HUMAN RIGHTS CONTEXT

THE DEATH PENALTY is cruel and inhuman and its use in the United States is racist, discriminatory and arbitrary. This is not only true in a judicial context; there is another context in which we must ask, what should the laws be; how must the laws be implemented? These questions must be posed equally in the historical context of the development of the culture of human rights.

The evolution of the concept and the guarantee of human rights, and the recognition of new forms of rights, such as the right to development, to the solidarity among peoples, are incompatible with the possibility of a state violating the most fundamental of all rights, the right to life. That being the case, the reservations made by the United States to Articles 6 and 7 of the International Covenant on Civil and Political Rights must be invalid, as they violate the nature and the purpose of that instrument, and are incompatible with the right to life stated in it.[1]

I come from Brazil where agents of the state kill without judicial proceedings inside the prisons, and the same agents of the state execute children, poor people and black people, extra-judicially.

BELISARIO DOS SANTOS, JR. Attorney, Sao Paulo; Member of the Comissao Justica e Paz da Arquidiocese de Sao Paulo; Comissao Nacional de Direitos Humanos da Ordem dos Advogados do Brasil; Associacao Internacional de Juristas Democratas; Comission de Expertos Por La Prevencion de la Tortura en Las Americas-Cepta; Associacao de Advogados Lat. Noamericanos Pela Defesa Dos Direitos Humanos Aala; Human Rights Missions to Argentina, Angola, Chile, Paraguay, Peru and Uruguay.

The death penalty is not efficient....It is incompatible with human rights. Its existence misdirects efforts, time and resources from areas that require our attention: the struggles against racism, violence and poverty.

Yet the target populations are the majority. Perhaps the difference is that in Brazil this still remains a crime.

However, I don't know which is worse, the hypocrisy before the systematic immunity of the killers or the perversion of a judicial system which, because of several technicalities, allows executions with racist juries, inexperienced attorneys, and the conviction of innocent people in a game that is more political than judicial.

Beyond the ethical and moral and judicial arguments, we must confront the myths that sustain public opinion. Is the death penalty efficient? Is its application in conformity with the quality of the laws? Does the death penalty reduce criminality? Are there other alternatives?

The death penalty is not efficient. There are alternatives. It is incompatible with human rights. Its existence misdirects efforts, time and resources from areas that require our attention: the struggles against racism, violence and poverty. For all these reasons, it must be abolished.

NOTES

[1] *International Covenant on Civil and Political Rights*, (1976) 999 U.N.T.S. 171; Multilateral Treaties, Reservations, Understandings, and Declarations, deposited with the Secretary General, status as of December 31, 1992, st/leg/ser.e/11, p. 132.

FRANCIS T. SEOW

RESPONSE TO THE DEATH PENALTY AS PRACTICED IN THE UNITED STATES

This decision is written in amplification of the extempore decision delivered at the conclusion of the Commission of Inquiry into the Death Penalty in the United States of America, organized by Amnesty International USA, on August 7, 1993. The Commission was unique in its array of witnesses, from death-row survivors to law enforcement officers to prosecutors, among others, whose disparateness, however, was linked by the common thread of personal or professional interest in this vexing question.

Among the many prominent witnesses who testified was Sonia Jacobs, a death-row survivor, who recounted with quiet eloquence her legal travails wherein both she and her husband, Jesse Tafero, were tried for murder, inadequately defended, convicted and condemned to death. When she was subsequently vindicated, her husband had already been executed. Professor Hugo Bedau of Tufts University, Boston, submitted that the evidence which had "freed Sonia Jacobs was tantamount to evidence that Jessie Tafero was innocent. It cannot be the case that the courts were correct in freeing Sonia and correct in executing Jessie."[1] Their case illustrates graphically the terrible finality of a death sentence,

FRANCIS T. SEOW Barrister-at-law (Middle Temple, London), Advocate & Solicitor; Visiting Fellow, East Asian Legal Studies, Harvard Law School. Non-constituency Member of Parliament, Singapore, 1988. Political detainee, and Amnesty International's Prisoner of Conscience, 1988. President of the Law Society of Singapore, 1985-86. Author of: *To Catch A Tartar: A Dissident in Lee Kuan Yew's Prison*, Yale University SEAS Monographs, September 21, 1994; *Media Enthralled: Singapore Revisited*, Westview Press (forthcoming).

"...It cannot be the case that the courts were correct in freeing Sonia and correct in executing Jessie." Their case illustrates graphically the terrible finality of a death sentence, and the lack of safeguards necessary to prevent miscarriages of justice.

and the lack of safeguards necessary to prevent miscarriages of justice.

Another witness, Walter McMillian, a black businessman, told [in testimony delivered before the U.S. Senate Judiciary Committee April 1, 1993][2] of a perverse accusation against him of the murder of a white girl in Monroe County, Alabama, of which he was totally innocent. Nonetheless, he was arrested, and charged.

Prosecuting counsels in the case conceded to Mr. McMillian's attorney "off the record" their belief that McMillian was innocent of the offense. Although the personal belief of counsel in the guilt or innocence of an accused person is generally irrelevant, given the circumstances in this particular case, it was bizarre that none of them saw fit to order further investigations. What possible satisfaction could anyone derive from seeing an innocent man executed? However that may be, McMillian testified that, for a year before he was ever tried for the alleged offense of murder, he was improperly detained on death row during which time he had perforce to witness several executions. He spent a total of six years on death row. Walter McMillian was finally vindicated, unlike others who were placed in a similar predicament.

Attorney Marlene Kamish said her client, Manuel Salazar, was charged with and convicted of murdering a police officer in Joliet, Illinois. Salazar allegedly had been brutally assaulted by the deceased who "attempted to kill him"[3] with his drawn gun. In the ensuing struggle for its possession, the gun accidentally went off and killed the police officer. Salazar himself had a gun which he had earlier used for "target shooting" but had thrown away when the deceased pursued him, and was at the material time unarmed, an important testimony to the state of his mind then. The deceased officer, who had been drinking while on duty, was discovered later to have a concealed knife strapped to his leg. There was no suggestion that it was an official issue. Salazar is now on death row in Pontiac, Illinois, pending appeal against his conviction to the Illinois Supreme Court.[4]

Sonia Jacobs, Walter McMillian, and other witnesses, gave their evidence with sincerity and passion, the totality of which indicts the American criminal justice system. It is noted that many of the cases to which we were referred were from the Southern states. In any event, it is abundantly clear from the evidence that the quality of defense lawyers who represent poor or indigent defendants is, as the witnesses repeatedly testified, a central issue to the problem.

Thomas Johnson, a former prosecutor in Minneapolis, Minnesota, and now in private law practice, said that in most states throughout the United States, the prosecutor is an elected official, whose decision in any capital case triggers the seeking of the death penalty, without which there would be no death-penalty prosecution.[5] The decision is a political one, dictated by promises that prosecutor had made during an election campaign, or by whatever cases have preceded it within the office. Has there, for example, been a significant case lost recently, and a prosecutor who might be seeking to regain public confidence? Perhaps, most importantly, the way in which the case is portrayed within the media is a very significant factor.

In Alabama all judges, both trial and appellate judges, run for reelection every six years. According to Stephen Bright, director of the Southern Center for Human Rights, Atlanta, Georgia, when that occurs, "judicial boundaries are drawn in such a way as to dilute the minority vote in order to keep minorities from being judges in these places."[6] The appointments of judges and prosecutors are closely intertwined. In most Southern states, there is no public defender system or organized system for providing competent legal representation for poor defendants. The appointment is made by local judges of a member of the bar —somewhat similar to the old English dock brief. The appointment of inexperienced or incompetent defense lawyers in capital cases by judges with a private or political agenda raises grave questions as to the character of the appointment process. In the circumstances, it is not at all surprising that many court-appointed lawyers do not "necessarily have any commitment to the clients, the issues or any understanding of them."[7] Some lawyers in the course of the trial were said to be drunk and incapable, or on drugs and burdened with personal problems to the extent that they could not function effectively as counsel. The system, such as it is, is compounded by lack of funds to engage competent and qualified specialists or by the duplicity of prosecuting counsel withholding evidence favorable to the defense. Thus, the task of ensuring that justice is done in capital cases becomes almost insuperable, an unsatisfactory state of affairs which impinges on the integrity of the entire criminal judicial system. Stephen Bright observed that "poor people accused of crimes do not pick their lawyers — they are stuck with their lawyers, and any mistakes that the lawyer makes in the process is held against the person accused, not against the lawyer."[8]

There is an understandable pressure on law enforcement officers by society and politicians to bring offenders to justice, especially in egregious cases. Unlike in England and some other Commonwealth countries, where the recommendation of a jury is given due consideration and respect, statutory law [in a few states] apparently allows a judge in America to overrule a jury's verdict of life imprisonment and impose the death penalty. We were also surprised to hear that it is not unconstitutional to execute someone with mental retardation or someone who was under 18 years of age at the time of the offense.

...we were left with the uneasy feeling that innocent persons are being periodically and wrongfully convicted of murder, and executed, and that there are not sufficient safeguards in the American criminal justice system to prevent such miscarriages of justice—a state of affairs which would have horrified not only the celebrated English jurist, Sir William Blackstone, but also the American public if only the true scope of the problem were better known.

Permeating the entire evidence throughout the two days of hearing was the recurrent dark theme of race and color, which should not, but does play, a significant part in the administration of American justice. The tales we heard were so incredible that Florizelle O'Connor was moved to remark that but for the truth the "stories ... sound like fiction."[9]

Many other death-penalty related issues were raised during the hearing, which are important but nonetheless subordinate to the all-encompassing question as to whether or not capital punishment should be abolished in the United States.

At the conclusion of the hearing, we were left with the uneasy feeling that innocent persons are being periodically and wrongfully convicted of murder, and executed, and that there are not sufficient safeguards in the American criminal justice system to prevent such miscarriages of justice—a state of affairs which would have horrified not only the celebrated English jurist, Sir William Blackstone,[10] but also the American public if only the true scope of the problem were better known. On the cumulative evidence as presented, I am of the view that a *prima facie* case has been made out for the abolition of the death penalty.

NOTES

[1] see Hugo Bedau, "Innocence and the Death Penalty," this issue.

[2] see Walter McMillian, Testimony given before U.S. Senate, Judiciary Committee, April 1, 1993, this issue.

[3] see Marlene Kamish, "The Case of Manuel Salazar," this issue.

[4] On September 22, 1994, the Illinois Supreme Court granted Manuel Salazar a new trial.

[5] see Thomas Johnson, "When Prosecutors Seek the Death Penalty," this issue.

[6] see Stephen Bright, "Race, Poverty and Disadvantage in the Infliction of the Death Penalty in the Death Belt," this issue.

[7] Ibid.

[8] Ibid.

[9] Florizelle O'Connor, remarks, Amnesty International Commission of Inquiry into the Death Penalty, August 7, 1993.

[10] Author of the famous dictum, "It is better that ten guilty persons escape than one innocent suffer."

BACRE WALY NDIAYE

THE U.S., THE U.N., AND ARBITRARY EXECUTIONS

UNLIKE the battlefields of the former Yugoslavia, or the green hills of Rwanda, or the mountains of Peru, the United States hardly appears to be a scene of human rights violations. But, the testimony presented at the Amnesty International Commission of Inquiry into the Death Penalty in the United States of America reflects serious human rights concerns.

The United States is not perceived abroad as the land of the death penalty, the land of unfair trials, the land of still deeply rooted discrimination. On the contrary, the United States attracts millions of immigrants and bears the dreams of billions of human beings all around the world.

How many people were impressed by measures taken by the United States, including, upon occasion, military action, to protect the lives of their citizens abroad? How many political opponents of dictatorial regimes have sought refuge in U.S. embassies? How many human rights organizations have been funded by U.S.-based foundations?

BACRE WALY NDIAYE Special Rapporteur on Extrajudicial, Summary or Arbitrary Executions for the Geneva-based United Nations Commission on Human Rights. Lawyer in private practice in Senegal. Founder member, Senegalese Section of Amnesty International (AI), 1980. Served as member of AI International Executive Committee (1985-1991). Founder member (1977) and Secretary-General (1979-1982), then chairperson (1982-1985) of the Senegalese Young Lawyers Association. Founder member of the Inter-African Lawyers Union (1980), the Human Rights Institute of the Dakar Bar and of the International Conference of French-Speaking Bar Associations.

The United States is not perceived abroad as the land of the death penalty, the land of unfair trials, the land of still deeply rooted discrimination.

Indeed, during the U.N. World Conference on Human Rights in 1993 in Vienna, the United States was not on the side of those countries claiming the right to specificity rather than universality of human rights. The work of Amnesty International USA will help many people to appreciate how far the human rights prescriptions of this single superpower are for external use only.

As the Special Rapporteur on the Extrajudicial, Summary or Arbitrary Executions of the United Nations Commission on Human Rights based in Geneva, my role as both an independent expert and a practicing lawyer in Senegal is to monitor and promote the application of internationally recognized standards aimed at protecting the right to life. My mandate is: deaths in detention or in police custody; deaths due to the use of force by law enforcement officials; violations of the right to life in armed conflicts; *refoulement* of people to a country where their lives are at risk; and violations of the right to life linked to the imposition and application of the death penalty.

In these respects my concerns are twofold: first, observance of international standards of fair trial wherever the death penalty is imposed; second, laws leading to the application of the death penalty. What I have tried to do since I took office in July 1992, is to reaffirm that the right to life is the most fundamental human right, the condition for enjoying all the others. To this end, only the highest standards of a fair trial, as set out in the International Covenant on Civil and Political Rights, are acceptable.

In fact, with the death penalty being a political expediency, the basic standards of a fair trial are almost never met. Many regimes cannot afford an independent tribunal with qualified judges. They cannot afford an open trial which ensures respect for the rights of defense. They cannot afford to guarantee due process, and the right of appeal is often ignored.

For instance, in Rwanda, hundreds of prisoners have been sentenced to death without any assistance from a lawyer. No Bar Association exists, and the government itself has publicly recognized that the judiciary is poorly trained and subject to corruption and political pressure. Therefore, despite a situation of *de facto* abolition in the country, in contrast to the very high number of extrajudicial executions, my recommendation was to suspend, at the very least, the imposition of the death penalty pending the institution of a constitutionally sound judiciary system.[1]

In many cases it is not the overall system which is substandard, but the branch made up of special judges with special procedures leading to predictable death sentences. Egypt is a good illustration of that.

Article 6 of the International Covenant on Civil and Political Rights has been interpreted by the U.N. Human Rights Committee and considered by the United Nations General Assembly as, "a minimum standard of legal guarantees for the protection of the right to life."[2] I have considered that this Article and its interpretation are to be taken as a rule of customary international law.

According to the Human Rights Committee, the death penalty has to be considered only for the most grave crimes and should be an exceptional measure. Therefore, I have suggested that my mandate should include a review of legislation aiming to widen the scope of the death penalty.

As the Human Rights Committee clearly has also reaffirmed the desirability of abolition of the death penalty,[3] I have suggested that all measures which are contrary to the desirability of abolition have to be carefully monitored by the U.N. Human Rights Commission. In this respect, deep concerns have been expressed about laws in China and executions of juvenile offenders in the United States and in Saudi Arabia and of executions of mentally ill people in the United States of America. The United Nations Human Rights Commission has endorsed this approach in a resolution on extrajudicial executions adopted in 1993.[4] I also denounced the prospect of reintroduction of the death penalty in Peru in a press conference in June 1993 in Lima, pending publication of my report on my visit to that country.

In the United States, the Government has claimed, following my repeated appeals on death penalty cases, that, "It does not be-

The death penalty is the United States' "secret garden," or rather the United States' "secret backyard." The decision on whether to use the death penalty illustrates the way a people considers itself, either as a human community which cares for those who fail or as a merciless group where the stronger crush the weaker to death.

lieve that the right to life guaranteed by the Universal Declaration precludes capital punishment in appropriate cases and under appropriate procedures."[5] The Government also stated that, "Article 6 of the Covenant expressly permits capital punishment."[6]

According to the U.S. Government, "Capital punishment does not violate a person's inalienable right to life or constitute cruel, inhuman or degrading punishment, at least as those terms are understood by parties to international human rights treaties."[7] The Government has argued, "In the United States, as in all democratic societies, penal law and sanctions should—and generally do—reflect the will of the people. In the United States, the people of the majority of our states and of the country as a whole demonstrated through the democratic process that they favor the possibility of capital punishment in cases involving aggravated crimes of murder, and federal law authorizes capital punishment. While the people of some states have chosen to abolish the death penalty, others have chosen to retain it."[8]

The United States Government has been silent on specific cases. Coming from a different cultural background, I fail to understand why federal laws should not be based on the highest standards of the country and why the federal state has decided to follow the retentionist states. The prospect of abolition of the death penalty in the United States is a task for the overall human rights movement as it will have effects on many other countries.

The death penalty is the United States' "secret garden," or rather the United States' "secret backyard." The decision on whether to use the death penalty illustrates the way a people considers itself, either as a human community which cares for those who fail or as a merciless group where the stronger crush the weaker to death. It indicates where the real value of human life stands.

The death penalty is also about the very nature of the state. Totalitarian measures are for totalitarian systems. Therefore, efforts have to be made not only by nongovernmental organizations but also by intergovernmental organizations, especially the United Nations, to outlaw the death penalty as a measure incompatible with the values of tolerance, dignity, and integrity, enshrined in the Universal Declaration of Human Rights. The international community should move from the desirability of abolition of the death penalty to the complete abolition of the death penalty.

Gambia is a small West African state almost included in Senegal. It contains maybe half a million inhabitants, 90 percent of them Muslim. Gambia abolished the death penalty in February 1993, because it considers the death penalty incompatible with the values of a democratic society and of a modern state. I hope the work of Amnesty International will allow the American people to soon reach the same conclusion.

NOTES

[1] Report by the Special Rapporteur on the Extrajudicial, Summary or Arbitrary Executions of the United Nations Commission on Human Rights, on his visit to Rwanda from April 8-17, 1993 (U.N. Doc. E/CN.4/1994/7/Add.1 at 21).

[2] Human Rights Committee General Comment 6, Article 6 (Sixteenth Session, 1982) in U.N. Doc. HRI/GEN/1, at 5 (1992); see also David Weissbrodt, "International Measures Against Arbitrary Killings by Governments," 77 *Proc. Am. Soc. Int'l Law* 378, 379-80 (1983).

[3] Human Rights Committee General Comment 6, Article 6 (Sixteenth Session, 1982) in U.N. Doc. HRI/GEN/1, at 6 (1992).

[4] C.H.R. res. 1994/82 of 9 March 1994; see also U.N. Doc. E/CN.4/1994/7 (1994); U.N. Doc. E/CN.4 1993/46 (1993); see also David Weissbrodt, "Execution of Juvenile Offenders by the United States Violates International Human Rights Law," 3 *Am. U.J. Int'l L. & Policy* 339 (1988).

[5] Letter from the Representative of the U.S.A. to the European Office of the U.N., Geneva, of February 8, 1993, p.2.

[6] Ibid.

[7] Ibid., p.8.

[8] Ibid., pp.7-8.

APPENDIX

UNIVERSAL DECLARATION OF HUMAN RIGHTS (EXTRACTS)

ADOPTED AND PROCLAIMED BY GENERAL ASSEMBLY RESOLUTION 217A (III) OF 10 DECEMBER 1948

PREAMBLE

Whereas recognition of the inherent dignity and of the equal and inalienable rights of all members of the human family is the foundation of freedom, justice and peace in the world,

Whereas disregard and contempt for human rights have resulted in barbarous acts which have outraged the conscience of mankind, and the advent of a world in which human beings shall enjoy freedom of speech and belief and freedom from fear and want has been proclaimed as the highest aspiration of common people,

Whereas it is essential, if man is not to be compelled to have recourse, as a last resort, to rebellion against tyranny and oppression, that human rights should be protected by the rule of law,

Whereas it is essential to promote the development of friendly relations between nations,

Whereas the peoples of the United Nations have in the Charter reaffirmed their faith in fundamental human rights, in the dignity and worth of the human person and in the equal rights of men and women and have determined to promote social progress and better standards of life in larger freedom,

Whereas Member States have pledged themselves to achieve, in co-operation with the United Nations, the promotion of universal respect for and observance of human rights and fundamental freedoms,

Whereas a common understanding of these rights and freedoms is of the greatest importance for the full realization of this pledge,

Now, therefore, the General Assembly Proclaims...

Article 3

Everyone has the right to life, liberty, and security of person.

Article 5

No one shall be subjected to torture or to cruel, inhuman or degrading treatment or punishment.

SIXTH PROTOCOL TO THE EUROPEAN CONVENTION ON HUMAN RIGHTS

PROTOCOL NO. 6

TO THE CONVENTION FOR THE PROTECTION OF HUMAN RIGHTS AND FUNDAMENTAL FREEDOMS CONCERNING THE ABOLITION OF THE DEATH PENALTY (EXTRACTS)

The member States of the Council of Europe, signatory to this Protocol to the Convention for the Protection of Human Rights and Fundamental Freedoms, signed at Rome on 4 November 1950 (hereinafter referred to as "the Convention");

Considering that the evolution that has occured in several member States of the Council of Europe expresses a general tendency in favour of abolition of the death penalty;

Have agreed as follows:

Article 1

The death penalty shall be abolished. No one shall be condemned to such penalty or executed.

Article 2

A State may make provision in its law for the death penalty in respect of acts committed in time of war or of imminent threat of war; such penalty shall be applied only in the instances laid down in the law and in accordance with its provisions. The State shall communicate to the Secretary General of the Council of Europe the relevant provisions of that law.

Article 3

No derogation from the provisions of this Protocol shall be made under Article 15 of the Convention.

Article 4

No reservation may be made under Article 64 of the Convention in respect of the provisions of this Protocol.

INTERNATIONAL COVENANT ON CIVIL AND POLITICAL RIGHTS (EXTRACTS)

ADOPTED AND OPENED FOR SIGNATURES, RATIFICATION AND ACCESSION BY U.N. GENERAL ASSEMBLY RESOLUTION 2200 A (XXI) OF 16 DECEMBER 1966

ENTRY INTO FORCE: MARCH 23, 1976

PART III

Article 6

1. Every human being has the inherent right to life. This right shall be protected by law. No one shall be arbitrarily deprived of his life.

2. In countries which have not abolished the death penalty, sentence of death may be imposed only for the most serious crimes in accordance with the law in force at the time of the commission of the crime and not contrary to the provisions of the present Covenant and to the Convention on the Prevention and Punishment of the Crime of Genocide. This penalty can only be carried out pursuant to a final judgement rendered by a competent court.

3. When deprivation of life constitutes the crime of genocide, it is understood that nothing in this article shall authorize any State Party to the present Covenant to derogate in any way from any obligation assumed under the provisions of the Convention on the Prevention and Punishment of the Crime of Genocide.

4. Anyone sentenced to death shall have the right to seek pardon or commutation of sentence. Amnesty, pardon or commutation of the sentence of death may be granted in all cases.

5. Sentence of death shall not be imposed for crimes committed by persons below eighteen years of age and shall not be carried out on pregnant women.

6. Nothing in this article shall be invoked to delay or to prevent the abolition of capital punishment by any State Party to the present Covenant.

Article 7

No one shall be subjected to torture or to cruel, inhuman or degrading treatment or punishment. In particular, no one shall be subjected without his free consent to medical or scientific experimentation.

Article 14

1. All persons shall be equal before the courts and tribunals. In the determination of any criminal charge against him, or of his rights and obligations in a suit at law, everyone shall be entitled to a fair and public hearing by a competent, independent and impartial tribunal established by law. The Press and the public may be excluded

from all or part of a trial for reasons of morals, public order (*ordre public*) or national security in a democratic society, or when the interest of the private lives of the parties so requires, or to the extent strictly necessary in the opinion of the court in special circumstances where publicity would prejudice the interests of justice; but any judgement rendered in a criminal case or in a suit at law shall be made public except where the interest of juvenile persons otherwise requires or the proceedings concern matrimonial disputes of the guardianship of children.

2. Everyone charged with a criminal offence shall have the right to be presumed innocent until proved guilty according to law.

3. In the determination of any criminal charge against him, everyone shall be entitled to the following minimum guarantees, in full equality:

(a) To be informed promptly and in detail in a language which he understands of the nature and cause of the charge against him;

(b) To have adequate time and facilities for the preparation of his defence and to communicate with counsel of his own choosing;

(c) To be tried without undue delay;

(d) To be tried in his presence, and to defend himself in person or through legal assistance of his own choosing; to be informed, if he does not have legal assistance, of this right; and to have legal assistance assigned to him, in any case where the interests of justice so require, and without payment by him in any such case if he does not have sufficient means to pay for it;

(e) To examine, or have examined, the witnesses against him and to obtain the attendance and examination of witnesses on his behalf under the same conditions as witnesses against him;

(f) To have the free assistance of an interpreter if he cannot understand or speak the language used in court;

(g) Not to be compelled to testify against himself or to confess guilt.

4. In the case of juvenile persons, the procedure shall be such as will take account of their age and the desirability of promoting their rehabilitation.

5. Everyone convicted of a crime shall have the right to his conviction and sentence being reviewed by a higher tribunal according to law.

6. When a person has by a final decision been convicted of a criminal offence and when subsequently his conviction has been reversed or he has been pardoned on the ground that a new or newly discovered fact shows conclusively that there has been a miscarriage of justice, the person who has suffered punishment as a result of such conviction shall be compensated according to law, unless it is proved that the non-disclosure of the unknown fact in time is wholly or partly attributable to him.

7. No one shall be liable to be tried or punished again for an offence for which he has already been finally convicted or acquitted in accordance with the law and penal procedure of each country.

SECOND OPTIONAL PROTOCOL TO THE INTERNATIONAL COVENANT ON CIVIL AND POLITICAL RIGHTS AIMING AT THE ABOLITION OF THE DEATH PENALTY (EXTRACTS)

UN GENERAL ASSEMBLY RESOLUTION 44/128 15 DECEMBER 1989

The States parties to the present Protocol,

Believing that abolition of the death penalty contributes to enhancement of human dignity and progressive development of human rights,

Recalling article 3 of the Universal Declaration of Human Rights adopted on 10 December 1948 and article 6 of the International Covenant on Civil and Political Rights adopted on 16 December 1966,

Noting that article 6 of the International Covenant on Civil and Political Rights refers to abolition of the death penalty in terms which strongly suggest that abolition is desirable,

Convinced that all measures of abolition of the death penalty should be considered as progress in the enjoyment of the right to life,

Desirous to undertake hereby an international commitment to abolish the death penalty,

Have Agreed as follows:

Article 1

1. No one within the jurisdiction of a State party to the present Optional Protocol shall be executed.

2. Each State party shall take all necessary measures to abolish the death penalty within its jurisdiction.

Article 2

1. No reservation is admissible to the present Protocol except for a reservation made at the time of ratification or accession which provides for the application of the death penalty in time of war pursuant to a conviction for a most serious crime of a military nature committed during wartime.

2. The State party making such a reservation will at the time of ratification or accession communicate to the Secretary-General of the United Nations the relevant provisions of its national legislation applicable during wartime.

3. The State party having made such a reservation will notify the Secretary-General of the United Nations of any beginning or ending of a state of war applicable to its territory.

SAFEGUARDS GUARANTEEING PROTECTION OF THE RIGHTS OF THOSE FACING THE DEATH PENALTY

ADOPTED BY THE UN ECONOMIC AND SOCIAL COUNCIL IN RESOLUTION 1984/50 AT ITS 1984 SPRING SESSION ON 25 MAY 1984 AND ENDORSED BY THE UN GENERAL ASSEMBLY IN RESOLUTION 39/118, ADOPTED WITHOUT A VOTE ON 14 DECEMBER 1984

1. In countries which have not abolished the death penalty, capi-

tal punishment may be imposed only for the most serious crimes, it being understood that their scope should not go beyond intentional crimes, with lethal or other extremely grave consequences.

2. Capital punishment may be imposed only for a crime for which the death penalty is prescribed by law at the time of its commission, it being understood that if, subsequent to the commission of the crime, provision is made by law for the imposition of a lighter penalty, the offender shall benefit thereby.

3. Persons below 18 years of age at the time of the commission of the crime shall not be sentenced to death, nor shall the death penalty be carried out on pregnant women, or on new mothers or on persons who have become insane.

4. Capital punishment may be imposed only when the guilt of the person charged is based upon clear and convincing evidence leaving no room for an alternative explanation of the facts.

5. Capital punishment may only be carried out pursuant to a final judgment rendered by a competent court after legal process which gives all possible safeguards to ensure a fair trial, at least equal to those contained in Article 14 of the International Covenant on Civil and Political Rights, including the right of anyone suspected of or charged with a crime for which capital punishment may be imposed to adequate legal assistance at all stages of the proceedings.

6. Anyone sentenced to death shall have the right to appeal to a court of higher jurisdiction, and steps should be taken to ensure that such appeals shall become mandatory.

7. Anyone sentenced to death shall have the right to seek pardon, or commutation of sentence; pardon or commutation of sentence may be granted in all cases of capital punishment.

8. Capital punishment shall not be carried out pending any appeal or other recourse procedure or other proceeding relating to pardon or commutation of the sentence.

9. Where capital punishment occurs, it shall be carried out so as to inflict the minimum possible suffering.

IMPLEMENTATION OF THE SAFEGUARDS GUARANTEEING PROTECTION OF THE RIGHTS OF THOSE FACING THE DEATH PENALTY (EXTRACTS)

RESOLUTION 1989/64, ADOPTED BY THE UNITED NATIONS ECONOMIC AND SOCIAL COUNCIL ON 24 MAY 1989

The Economic and Social Council,

Recalling its resolution 1984/50 of 25 May 1984, containing safeguards for those facing the death penalty,

Also recalling resolution 15 of the Seventh Congress on the Prevention of Crime and the Treatment of Offenders,

Further recalling Council resolution 1986/10, section X, of 21 May 1986, in which the Council requested a study of the death penalty and new contributions from the criminal sciences to the matter,

Noting the report of the Secretary-General on the implementation of the safeguards,

Also noting with satisfaction that a large number of Member States have provided the Secretary-General with information on the implementation of the safeguards and have made contributions,

Further noting with appreciation the study on the question of the death penalty and the new contributions of the criminal sciences to the matter,

Alarmed at the continued occurrence of practices incompatible with the safeguards guaranteeing protection of the rights of those facing the death penalty,

Convinced that further progress should be achieved towards more effective implementation of the safeguards at a national level on the understanding that they shall not be invoked to delay or to prevent the abolition of capital punishment,

Acknowledging the need for comprehensive and accurate information and additional research about the implementation and the safeguards and the death penalty in general in every region of the world,

1. *Recommends* that Member States take steps to implement the safeguards and strengthen further the protection of the rights of those facing the death penalty, where applicable, by:

(a) Affording special protection to persons facing charges for which the death penalty is provided by allowing time and facilities for the preparation of their defence, including the adequate assistance of counsel at every stage of the proceedings, above and beyond the protection afforded in non-capital cases;

(b) Providing for mandatory appeals or review with provisions for clemency or pardon in all cases of capital offence;

(c) Establishing a maximum age beyond which a person may not be sentenced to death or executed;

(d) Eliminating the death penalty for persons suffering from mental retardation or extremely limited mental competence, whether at the stage of sentence or execution;

2. *Invites* Member States to co-operate with the specialized bodies, non-governmental organizations, academic institutions and specialists in the field in efforts to conduct research on the use of the death penalty in every region of the world;

3. *Also invites* Member States to facilitate the efforts of the Secretary-General to gather comprehensive, timely and accurate information about the implementation of the safeguards and the death penalty in general;

4. *Invites* Member States that have not yet done so to review the extent to which their legislation provides for the safeguards guaranteeing protection of the rights of those facing the death penalty as set out in the annex to Economic and Social Council resolution 1984/50 of 25 May 1984;

5. *Urges* Member States to publish, for each category of offence for which the death penalty is authorized, and if possible on an

annual basis, information about the use of the death penalty, including the number of persons sentenced to death, the number of executions actually carried out, the number of persons under sentence of death, the number of death sentences reversed or commuted on appeal and the number of instances in which clemency has been granted, and to include information on the extent to which the safeguards referred to above are incorporated in national law;

6. *Recommends* that the report of the Secretary-General on the question of capital punishment, to be submitted to the Economic and Social Council in 1990, in pursuance of resolution 1745 (LIV) of 16 May 1973, should henceforth cover the implementation of the safeguards as well as the use of capital punishment;

7. *Requests* the Secretary-General to publish the study on the death penalty and the new contributions of the criminal sciences to the matter prepared pursuant to Economic and Social Council resolution 1986/10, section X, paragraph 2 (b), and to make it available, with other relevant documentation, to the Eighth United Nations Congress on the Prevention of Crime and the Treatment of Offenders.

AMERICAN CONVENTION ON HUMAN RIGHTS (EXTRACT)

OPENED FOR SIGNATURE NOVEMBER 22, 1969

ENTRY INTO FORCE: JULY, 1978

Article 4. Right to Life

1. Every person has the right to have his life respected. This right shall be protected by law and, in general, from the moment of conception. No one shall be arbitrarily deprived of his life.

2. In countries that have not abolished the death penalty, it may be imposed only for the most serious crimes and pursuant to a final judgment rendered by a competent court and in accordance with a law establishing such punishment, enacted prior to the commis-

sion of the crime. The application of such punishment shall not be extended to crimes to which it does not presently apply.

3. The death penalty shall not be reestablished in states that have abolished it.

4. In no case shall capital punishment be inflicted for political offenses or related common crimes.

5. Capital punishment shall not be imposed upon persons who, at the time the crime was committed, were under 18 years of age or over 70 years of age; nor shall it be applied to pregnant women.

6. Every person condemned to death shall have the right to apply for amnesty, pardon, or commutation of sentence, which may be granted in all cases. Capital punishment shall not be imposed while such a petition is pending decision by the competent authority.

PROTOCOL TO THE AMERICAN CONVENTION ON HUMAN RIGHTS TO ABOLISH THE DEATH PENALTY

ADOPTED AND PROCLAIMED BY THE ORGANIZATION OF AMERICAN STATES AT THE TWENTIETH REGULAR SESSION OF THE GENERAL ASSEMBLY ON JUNE 8, 1990

PREAMBLE

The States Parties to this Protocol,

Considering:

That Article 4 of the American Convention on Human Rights recognizes the right to life and restricts the application of the death penalty;

That everyone has the inalienable right to respect for his life, a right that cannot be suspended for any reason;

That the tendency among the American States is to be in favor of abolition of the death penalty;

That application of the death penalty has irrevocable consequences, forecloses the correction of judicial error, and precludes any possibility of changing or rehabilitating those convicted;

That the abolition of the death penalty helps to ensure more effective protection of the right to life;

That an international agreement must be arrived at that will entail a progressive development of the American Convention on Human Rights, and

That States Parties to the American Convention on Human Rights have expressed their intention to adopt an international agreement with a view to consolidating the practice of not applying the death penalty in the Americas,

Have Agreed to Sign the Following Protocol to the American Convention on Human Rights to Abolish the Death Penalty

Article 1

The States Parties to this Protocol shall not apply the death penalty in their territory to any person subject to their jurisdiction.

Article 2

1. No reservations may be made to this Protocol. However, at the time of ratification or accession, the States Parties to this instrument may declare that they reserve the right to apply the death penalty in wartime in accordance with international law, for extremely serious crimes of a military nature.

2. The State Party making this reservation shall, upon ratification or accession, inform the Secretary General of the Organization of American States of the pertinent provisions of its national legislation applicable in wartime, as referred to in the preceding paragraph.

3. Said State Party shall notify the Secretary General of the Organization of American States of the beginning or end of any state of war in effect of its territory.

Article 3

This Protocol shall be open for signature and ratification or accession by any State Party to the American Convention on Human Rights.

Ratification of this Protocol or accession thereto shall be made through the deposit of an instrument of ratification or accession with the General Secretariat of the Organization of American States.

Article 4

This Protocol shall enter into force among the States that ratify or accede to it when they deposit their respective instruments of ratification or accession with the General Secretariat of the Organization of American States.

SIGNATORIES TO: INTERNATIONAL TREATIES ON THE DEATH PENALTY

INTERNATIONAL COVENANT ON CIVIL AND POLITICAL RIGHTS

Countries that have ratified/acceded:

Afghanistan, Albania, Algeria, Angola, Argentina, Armenia, Australia, Austria, Azerbaydzhan, Barbados, Belarus, Belgium, Benin, Bolivia, Bosnia-Herzegovina, Brazil, Bulgaria, Burundi, Cambodia, Cameroon, Canada, Cape Verde, Central African Republic, Chile, Colombia, Congo, Costa Rica, Cote d'Ivoire, Croatia, Cyprus, Czech Republic, Denmark, Dominica, Dominican Republic, Ecuador, Egypt, El Salvador, Equatorial Guinea, Estonia, Ethiopia, Finland, France, Gabon, Gambia, Germany, Grenada, Guatemala, Guinea, Guyana, Haiti, Hungary, Iceland, India, Iran, Iraq, Ireland, Israel, Italy, Jamaica, Japan, Jordan, Kenya, Korea (Democratic People's Republic), Korea (Republic of), Latvia, Lebanon, Lesotho, Libyan Arab Jamahiriya, Lithuania, Luxembourg, Madagascar, Malawi, Mali, Malta, Mauritius, Mexico, Moldova, Mongolia, Morocco, Mozambique, Nepal, Netherlands, New Zealand, Nicaragua, Niger, Nigeria, Norway, Panama, Paraguay, Peru, Philippines, Poland, Portugal, Romania, Russian Federation, Rwanda, St. Vincent and the Grenadines, San Marino, Senegal, Seychelles, Slovakia, Slovenia, Somalia, Spain, Sri Lanka, Sudan, Suriname, Sweden, Switzerland, Syrian Arab Republic, Tanzania, Togo, Trinidad and Tobago, Tunisia, Ukraine, United Kingdom, United States of America, Uruguay, Venezuela, Vietnam, Yemen, Yugoslavia (Federal Republic of), Zaire, Zambia, Zimbabwe

Countries that have signed but not yet ratified:

Honduras, Liberia

(as of December 31, 1993)

SECOND OPTIONAL PROTOCOL TO THE INTERNATIONAL COVENANT ON CIVIL AND POLITICAL RIGHTS

Countries that have ratified/acceded:
Australia, Austria, Denmark, Ecuador, Finland, Germany, Hungary, Iceland, Luxembourg, Netherlands, New Zealand, Norway, Panama, Portugal, Romania, Slovenia, Spain, Sweden, Uruguay, Venezuela

Countries that have signed but not yet ratified:
Belgium, Costa Rica, Honduras, Italy, Nicaragua

(as of February 1994)

SIXTH PROTOCOL TO THE EUROPEAN CONVENTION ON HUMAN RIGHTS

Countries that have ratified/acceded:
Austria, Czech Republic, Denmark, Finland, France, Germany, Hungary, Iceland, Italy, Liechtenstein, Luxembourg, Malta, Netherlands, Norway, Portugal, San Marino, Slovakia, Spain, Sweden, Switzerland

Countries that have signed but not yet ratified:
Belgium, Greece, Estonia, Romania, Slovenia

(as of February 1994)

AMERICAN CONVENTION ON HUMAN RIGHTS

Countries that have ratified/acceded:
Argentina, Barbados, Bolivia, Brazil, Chile, Colombia, Costa Rica, Dominica, Dominican Republic, Ecuador, El Salvador, Grenada, Guatemala, Haiti, Honduras, Jamaica, Mexico, Nicaragua, Panama, Paraguay, Peru, Suriname, Trinidad and Tobago,Uruguay, Venezuela

Countries that have signed but not yet ratified:
United States of America

(as of November 1, 1994)

PROTOCOL TO THE AMERICAN CONVENTION ON HUMAN RIGHTS TO ABOLISH THE DEATH PENALTY

Countries that have ratified/acceded:
Panama

Countries that have signed but not yet ratified:
Costa Rica, Ecuador, Nicaragua, Uruguay, Venezuela

(as of February 1994)

For more information
on Amnesty International's work
to abolish the death penalty
and to support human rights worldwide
write:

Amnesty International USA
322 Eighth Avenue
New York, New York 10001